# Change

### THE TOOLS YOU NEED

### FOR THE LIFE YOU WANT

### AT WORK AND HOME

———

## GARY BRADT

RIVER GROVE
BOOKS

Published by River Grove Books
Austin, TX
www.rivergrovebooks.com

Distributed by River Grove Books

Design and composition by Greenleaf Book Group and Kim Lance
Cover design by Greenleaf Book Group and Kim Lance

Cover image: 3dfoto/ iStock Collection/Thinkstock
Interior Circular Arrow Graph: Image Copyright corund, 2016.
Interior Sidewalk Flower: Image Copyright Poptika, 2016.
Used under license from Shutterstock.com

Cataloging-in-Publication data is available.

Print ISBN: 978-1-63299-114-0

eBook ISBN: 978-1-63299-115-7

First Edition

To the three professional mentors in my life: Dr. Kenneth Bradt, my father; Dr. Spencer Johnson, author of *Who Moved My Cheese?*; and Dr. Jim Farr, who hired me out of grad school and whose lessons still ring true today.

*You don't have time to read a book.*

*I didn't have time to write one.*

*This is a match made in heaven!*

# Contents

# Foreword

WE LIVE IN A Twitter world. We want practical content, and we want it fast. I wrote this book about change to acknowledge our busy lives.

This book promises to be a quick read with lasting impact. Inside you will find relatable stories and practical tools to help you adapt to and advance through changes at work and at home.

I hope you will pick it up whenever change hits and turns your world upside down.

Perhaps you will come to discover as I have that it's not the change in our lives, but how we choose to adapt to it, that makes all the difference.

# Introduction

"NOT AGAIN!" CHERYL GROANED as she pulled out of the school parking lot. *I'm gonna be late!*

She banged her hand on the wheel as the traffic in front of her stopped for no apparent reason, as it did almost every morning.

"Move, people, move!" she heard herself groan. Then, she glanced at her gas gauge and noticed she was running low. *Just what I need. A perfect start to a perfect day!*

Cheryl sighed. Her mind flashed to the chaos of the morning. It had become a stressful routine: waking up early to rouse the kids and then scurrying to help them get dressed. Then, Cheryl had to throw together some semblance of breakfast while hurriedly packing lunches. Her kids scrambled to find shoes, coats, and backpacks while they fussed with each other. Nobody got out the door on time.

Cheryl's husband, Edward, would normally help her out, but he was out of town. His travel for work had really picked up the last several months. *We hardly see each other anymore,* Cheryl thought. *It's like we have to schedule time on our calendars just to sit down to have an adult conversation.*

Between Edward's schedule and hers, it had gotten difficult. Their time together consisted mostly of late-night calls from Edward on the road, and then weekends packed with too much to do. They spent most of their time running the kids from one event to another and catching up on errands. Then Edward would hop on a plane Sunday evening, and it started all over again.

Cheryl sighed. *We don't have any time for ourselves. We can't keep this up. Something's gotta give.*

The traffic today was even slower than usual. Cheryl accepted that there was nothing she could do; she was going to be late to her job at Carson-Co again. As she waited at a red light, she closed her eyes and took a deep breath. Her phone broke her reverie; it sounded the distinctive ring for her parents.

*What is it?* she thought. *They never call this time of day.*

Cheryl's chest tightened as she picked up the call. "Mom?"

It wasn't Cheryl's mom. It was her dad.

"Cheryl, don't worry honey, it looks like everything is going to be okay, but your mother is in the hospital again. She got short of breath during the night and I took her to the ER," he said.

"How serious is it, Dad? Do you need me to come out there again?" Cheryl asked.

"No, no, that's okay, honey," her dad said. "No need to come out for now. The doctors think it's just a medication issue. They are running some tests and we'll see. I think she'll be okay."

"Are you sure? I can come out there if you need me to. I know this has to be getting hard for you, too," Cheryl said.

This was the third time Cheryl's father had taken her mom to the ER in the last several months.

"Well, thanks, honey, but I think I'm doing okay. I know you and Edward are busy with your jobs and the kids and all. We should be all right," her dad said. "I'll keep you posted and let you know if anything changes."

"Okay, Dad. Love you. Tell Mom I love her too," Cheryl said.

"Will do. Love you too, honey. Try not to worry! We'll be all right," her dad said as he hung up.

*Yeah, sure*, Cheryl thought. *Try not to worry!*

These kinds of calls were becoming more common. And troubling.

Cheryl had flown out twice recently for similar crises. Despite what her dad said, she wondered if she might have to go again soon.

Although she had siblings who said they would help out in times like this, they always seemed to be too busy when the time came. Mom and Dad had learned to call her when something went wrong.

*It's really beginning to strain our budget*, she thought. *If I go out there again, there goes whatever we've saved up for the family vacation this summer. But what can I do? I love them and they need me.*

By now traffic was finally moving again. Cheryl decided not to stop for gas. *I think I can make it. I'm late enough as it is.*

Cheryl pulled into a parking space, scrambled across the parking lot, and rushed upstairs. When she stepped in the office she felt a buzz in the air. Her colleagues were huddled in small groups and talking nervously.

"What's going on?" Cheryl asked the receptionist, Sarah. "What sort of mischief is corporate up to this time?"

Sarah wasn't smiling.

"Haven't you heard?" she asked.

"Heard what?" Cheryl replied, sensing her concern.

"Carson-Co has been sold," Sarah exclaimed. "Our biggest competitor bought us out!"

---

## The Change Journey

In our fast-moving world, change rarely slows. Sometimes it's change at work, and sometimes it's change at home. And often, like with Cheryl, it is both.

There are two types of change we will explore in this book: *External change* includes events that happen outside your control that are perhaps different from what you expected or wanted. *Internal change* is the process of making change happen by choosing better thoughts and behavior to get the results you want. Both types of change create opportunities. My goal is to give you the tools you need to unearth them.

Sometimes we can see change coming like a train in the distance. Other times—*wham*! Change is a lightning bolt out of the blue. In either case, change can be stressful and hard.

When change has interrupted your life, how do you adapt and advance to something better? This is the question we will answer in this book. We will also follow Cheryl and her colleagues at Carson-Co as they attempt to answer this question for themselves. In each chapter I will also share some real-life change stories, based on my experiences as a father, husband, executive coach, and speaker.

I hope some of the characters we will meet and their stories will resonate with you. Perhaps you will see yourself in them. Or maybe you will recognize someone you know at work or at home. Most importantly, I hope that as we watch others learn to adapt and advance in their lives, you will learn how to adapt and advance too.

We will also explore **nine tools** for leading yourself and others through change. The tools are ways of thinking, feeling, and behaving to get the results you want. These tools, like the book, are divided into three sections:

## PART 1:
## Managing Your Relationships Through Change

1. *Choose Your Response to Change:* We don't always get to choose change, but we always get to choose our response. The Roadmap is a tool to help you choose responses to get the results you want.

2. *Change Relationships by Changing Yourself:* You can't change anyone else, but you can change yourself and influence others to help create the relationships you want.

3. *Make a ToWho List*: Relationships are shock absorbers: They soften the blow of difficult change. Use your ToWho List to sustain relationships that matter most.

## PART 2:
## Managing Yourself Through Change

1. *Adapt First and Fast*: If you're not adapting, you're falling behind—and catching up is hard. Successful people and organizations get ahead by learning to adapt to change faster and better than everyone else.

2. *Let Go*: Holding on to regrets from the past or fears about the future will hinder you from grasping opportunities now.

3. *Latch On*: Values are like a compass. They point you in the right direction when change has you feeling lost and you are not sure which way to turn next.

## PART 3:
## Managing Change to Create the Life You Want

1. *Imagine the Life You Want*: Imagining the life you want helps you create it. Combining a passionate vision with patience and persistence is your key to long-term success.

2. *Grow Where You're Planted:* Leaders don't have time to complain about change. They are too busy doing something about it.

3. *Write Your Story:* You are the author of your life story. You don't always get to choose how your personal change story begins, but you get to choose how it ends.

I learned most of these tools throughout my lifetime. I learned them by being a father and husband, speaker and executive coach. I learned them by making mistakes and learning from them, too.

Most importantly, I've learned from people just like you. I have dedicated my career to helping others through change, and my clients have helped me learn and grow.

Now I want to share the tools I've learned with you.

In each chapter, we will—

- Watch how Cheryl and her colleagues at Carson-Co learn to apply the tools to adapt and advance, both at work and at home

- Dig a little deeper into the concepts behind the tools and share real-life stories to show how the tools can help you change too

- Offer questions and tips for application so you can turn your intentions into action

- Summarize each chapter's major points

At work, you may want to read this book as a team and discuss how applying the tools might help you meet the change challenges in your organization. At home, you may want to read it with someone you love and discuss how the tools might help you adapt and advance as a couple or as a family. Or you may choose to read it alone and reflect on how the tools can help you adapt to change in your life.

I want to help you go beyond simply coping with change. I want you to *thrive* through change. The tools will help you make that happen.

I hope you will turn to them again and again to create the results that you want, whenever change creates challenges in your life. And I hope you will share the tools with others too.

I truly believe that every change creates opportunities. It's up to you to find them. It's up to me to show you how.

PART ONE

# Managing
# Your Relationships
# Through Change

# One

# Choose Your Response to Change

JUSTIN WONDERED HOW HE would break the news to his wife and kids. He was still trying to digest it himself. After twenty-two years at Carson-Co, it was over. Just like that. He was called to a meeting and told his services were no longer needed.

A corporate exec named Ken was in the front of the room trying to explain it to Justin and the others. Something about market consolidation and the need to reduce expenses and duplicate services. It was hard to focus. Justin's mind raced. He hadn't seen this coming.

Oh, he knew changes were taking place in his industry. Competitors had been quicker to pick up on newer technologies than Carson-Co had. Carson-Co's products and services had fallen behind as a result.

But Justin had felt secure when the notice came that the company was being acquired. His division had been profitable. His department had been immune from the periodic layoffs—until now.

Justin blinked and tried to refocus. Ken was saying something about the severance package and going on about outplacement and extended benefits. Anger cracked through Justin like lightning.

*It's not fair! Twenty-two years, and for what?* He got up and walked quickly to the door. *I don't need this!*

Justin brushed past the Carson-Co HR rep and went straight to his office. He packed hastily. Thirty minutes later he was gone.

The following days passed in a blur. Justin refused outplacement, where career counselors could help him prepare a resume and look for a new job. Instead, he spent time talking with others who had been let go. Many were angry like him. The more they talked, the angrier they got.

A few, like his friend and colleague Brandon, were philosophical. They saw this as a chance for a fresh start. Justin thought they were naïve. Getting fired for no good reason was not his idea of a fresh start.

Justin eventually began looking for a new job on his own. He didn't expect any trouble. After all, his record was strong and his skills were up-to-date. Or so he thought.

Justin had kept up with his technical training at Carson-Co, but he hadn't bothered to take any of the soft-skills courses they offered. He was always too busy for something like that. *Why waste my time?* he thought.

As a result, Justin's technical skills were up-to-date, but his people skills lagged. His old-school mentality of "command and control" was out of synch with a business world that was increasingly relying on teamwork and collaboration.

When Justin interviewed, he made little effort to mask his attitude toward Carson-Co. They were foolish for letting him and the others go. They rid the company of too much experience. They were relying on kids and would pay a price for that down the line.

Justin thought his analysis demonstrated his experience and business savvy. But interviewers believed he had a negative attitude they did not want to bring into their company.

Justin did not get many second interviews and he received no offers. He was determined to never let a company get the best of him again. They didn't. No company wanted a piece of Justin at all.

*It's a tough economy*, he thought.

Time went by and nothing happened. Justin went on fewer interviews. He spent more time in his home office or tried to stay busy doing projects around the house. After a while it was hard to find enough to do.

The idleness began to gnaw at him. He began to worry. He had his kids' college tuition coming up and a mortgage to pay. His severance package was time limited. He hated to dip into savings, but it was beginning to look like he might have to.

Unwittingly, Justin began taking his frustrations out on his wife, Donna, and his kids. His temper was short. His sense of humor, gone. One day, after another major blowup over a minor violation, his youngest son ran from the room.

"I want my old dad back!" he cried, slamming the door behind him.

The sound of the slamming door hung in the air. A lone clock ticked in the corner. Justin stared at the closed door for a long time. Then he rubbed his eyes and wearily rested his head in his hands.

*Where do I go from here?*

### DIG A LITTLE DEEPER:

## You Don't Always Get to Choose Change, but You Always Get to Choose Your Response

Like Justin's, many people's initial reactions to change are predictable. *I can't believe this is happening. How can they do this? It's not fair. I'm going to fight it.*

These reactions are understandable. Our safe and predictable world has disappeared. Our routines are disrupted. We feel threatened, angry, and afraid.

Out of our feelings, we may begin acting against our own best interests.

When this happens, the critical question to ask is—

## Is my reaction to change getting me the results I want?[1]

If so, great. Keep it up. But if you find yourself in a place you'd rather not be (like Justin), perhaps it's time to make a change.

### THE ROADMAP:
### A Simple Tool to Help You Change

The *Roadmap* is a tool to help you change at work and in life. Like all maps, it helps you understand how you got to where you are and, more importantly, how to get to where you want to go next. We will refer to the Roadmap frequently as a tool for helping you adapt to and advance through change throughout the rest of this book.

---

1    A question I was taught to ask by Dr. Spencer Johnson, the author of the bestselling book on change: *Who Moved My Cheese? An Amazing Way to Deal with Change in Your Work and in Your Life.*

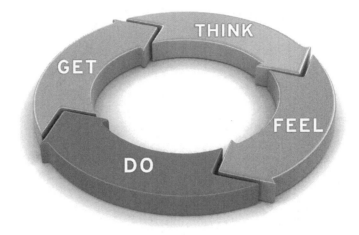

The Roadmap may help you understand why you do what you do, and it can help you change what you do to get better results. You read the Roadmap like a clock, starting at twelve o'clock, then moving clockwise.

The journey to results goes like this—

- *Thinking* triggers feelings.

- *Feelings* fuel behavior.

- *Behavior* determines *results*.

It's a circular process, therefore:

### The road to better results always begins with better thinking.

For example, let's look at Justin's Roadmap:

- *Thinking:* Carson-Co was wrong to let me go; this is unfair; I got a raw deal

- *Feelings:* Anger and betrayal

- *Behavior:* Refusing outplacement services; being negative in interviews; taking it out emotionally on my family

- *Results:* No job offers; frayed family relationships; a creeping sense of desperation

How might Justin change his thinking to get different results? A few possible answers come to mind. What if Justin adjusted his Roadmap to something like this?

- *Thinking:* Change is my opportunity to try something new; yes, this is hard, but I have gotten through tough changes before and I can do it again

- *Feelings:* A sense of hope and determination

- *Behavior:* Putting all my energy into finding a new job versus lamenting the one I lost

- *Results:* Discovering new opportunities

What other kinds of thoughts might he choose that could lead to better results? Perhaps you can write your answers down.

### *Change in Real Life: Using the Roadmap to Change Results*

One time, when my teenage son did something that really set me off—I don't even remember now what it was—I was ready to go upstairs and tell him what I thought he needed to know in no uncertain terms. Then, my wife, Peggy, intervened.

"What are you going to say to him?" she asked.

"I'm going to tell him what he did wrong and what he needs to know!" I barked.

Peggy asked, "If you go up there and say what you want to say, as angry as you are now, what will he hear? What will he think?"

I paused and took a deep breath.

"He'll hear and think that Dad is a jerk," I said with a sigh. "And he will have no clue that he did anything wrong."

This was clearly not the result that I wanted.

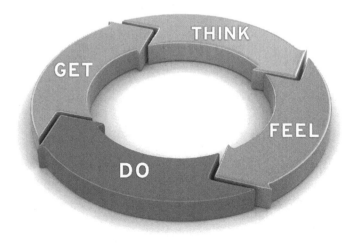

- *My Thinking:* He's not doing it right

- *My Feelings:* Anger

- *My Behavior:* Angry outburst

- *My Results:* Dad is a jerk

## If I wanted to change my results, I needed to change my thinking.

So after calming down, I changed my thinking to—

- *New Thinking:* I love my son and want to help him make better choices

- *New Feelings:* Love and concern

- *New Behavior:* A calm talk where I shared my concerns with him

- *New Results:* A productive outcome where we both felt heard and supported

To be clear, I wasn't immediately successful utilizing this approach consistently going forward. Sometimes I let my negative thinking and feelings in the moment overwhelm me, and I reverted to my old patterns. Changing behavior takes time, as we'll explore more in chapter seven. But I stuck with it and eventually the results I got with my son were closer to my intentions.

## Choosing "Want to" over "Have to"

With my son, I changed my behavior because I wanted to, not because I had to. Wanting to do something often produces better results than feeling like you have to.

## The Power of Choosing a Want-To Roadmap

There are two basic types of Roadmaps: *Want-To* and *Have-To*. Want-To Roadmaps encourage you to *run toward* something you want. Have-To Roadmaps encourage you to *run away* from something you don't. Want-To Roadmaps give you better results than Have-To Roadmaps.

For example, let's say your goal is to make change happen: You want to lose weight.

A Have-To Roadmap may be filled with Shoulds and Oughts and might look something like this:

- *Thinking:* I have to lose weight; I ought to eat better; I should exercise more

- *Feelings:* Resentment and frustration

- *Behavior:* Grudging compliance for a while, perhaps, followed by more and more "cheating," or eating and doing as you please

- *Results:* Falling short of your goals

Have-To Roadmaps are hard to sustain because they create internal mental barriers. It's like arm wrestling with yourself. A Want-To Roadmap creates no such barriers.

A Want-To Roadmap for losing weight might look like this:

- *Thinking:* I want to lose weight; I want to feel better and be healthier

- *Feelings:* Confidence and a determined commitment

- *Behavior:* Eating and exercising more in alignment with my goals, and not giving up the first time I slip up

- *Results:* A much better chance of hitting my target

Of course, choosing a Want-To Roadmap over a Have-To Roadmap doesn't guarantee results. But it may stack the odds in your favor, because it does not create unnecessary and self-defeating mental barriers.

Another common Roadmap for making change happen is the *All or Nothing Roadmap*, which falls into the Have-To Roadmap camp.

## The All or Nothing Roadmap

The All or Nothing Roadmap is a variation of a Have-To Roadmap. It's a "grind it out" mentality. True, good things can come from thinking this way. It sounds determined and feels powerful. But if you're not careful, exclusive use of this Roadmap can grind you up too.

For example, let's say you want to get ahead at work. Your All or Nothing Roadmap may look like this:

- *Thinking:* I am going to do whatever it takes to get ahead; I'll take every project, work harder and longer than everyone else; I'll never let up

- *Feelings:* Dogged determination followed by exhaustion or burnout

- *Behavior:* Running all out, every time, all the time

- *Results:* Hitting your goals? Maybe. But usually at a price, which often includes things like poor personal health or neglected relationships.

An alternative for attacking your goals might be an *All or Something Roadmap* that may go something like this:

- *Thinking:* I want to get ahead and will do whatever it takes, but not at the expense of my health or relationships

- *Feelings:* Confident determination and resolve

- *Behavior:* Hard work balanced by timeouts for you and time with those you care about

- *Results:* Gradual and sustainable success

No Roadmap can guarantee that you will reach your goals every time, but where you start impacts where you finish. You always get to determine where you start.

## QUESTIONS AND TIPS FOR APPLICATION

Now think about a change in your life that you are struggling with. Consider the following questions regarding that change. You may want to write your answers down.

- My thoughts about this change are—

_____
_____
_____
_____

- My feelings about this change are—

_____
_____
_____
_____

- What I have been doing in response to my feelings is—

_____
_____
_____
_____

- What I am getting as a result is—

_____
_____
_____
_____

Are you getting the results you want? If so, great. If not, to get a better result, try answering the questions below:

- How might I think differently about this change to get better results? (For example, if the change is at work, is this an opportunity to try something new or learn something new? If it is a personal change, is this an opportunity to support someone or allow others to support you? Either at home or at work, is this an opportunity to take a chance you've always wanted to take but have been too afraid to try before? Give yourself permission to dream!)

_____

_____

_____

_____


- How would I *like* to feel about this change? How might I use an *All or Something* mentality to help me feel that way?

_____

_____

_____

_____


- How might I change what I do as a result of changing how I think and feel?

_____

_____

_____

_____

- How might that behavior lead to better results?

_____

_____

_____

_____

Write down your answers to these questions and perhaps discuss them with a trusted friend or colleague. Then, act on what you wrote.

## CHOOSE YOUR RESPONSE TO CHANGE

- Better results start with better thinking.

- Changing how I think changes how I feel.

- Changing how I feel changes what I do.

- Changing what I do changes my results.

- I can't always control what happens, but I can always choose my response.

# Two

# Change Relationships by Changing Yourself

KIMBERLY'S MIND ROCKED BACK and forth like the wheels of the train she was riding home from work. *How did I end up here?*

Kimberly had joined Carson-Co right out of grad school. At first, coworkers experienced her as a breath of fresh air. She brought innovative ideas to a stagnating business. When given her own business unit to run, Kimberly succeeded beyond her wildest expectations. Her numbers exploded and customers loved her.

When it was announced that Carson-Co was being acquired, most assumed Kimberly would be a success in the new combined company too. After all, her reputation in the industry was golden.

Inside Carson-Co, however, it had become a different story, as her boss Ken had just shared with her.

"Your hyperfocus on your objectives means you some-times ignore the needs of others," Ken had told her. "You can be abrupt when communicating with your team. Too often, you talk more than listen. It's as if you're speeding down the highway with blinders on, and you don't notice the other cars on the road. You can run your colleagues over without realizing it."

Ken said that over time, Kimberly's attitude had grated on her team and many of her colleagues, and she had begun to pay the price.

"Too many people see you now as only out for yourself, Kimberly. Some of your peers don't want to work with you anymore, and some talented people on your team are start-ing to ask for transfers or are exploring their options outside the company. This simply can't continue."

As they discussed it, Ken admitted that he was part of the problem too.

"At first, I overlooked some of this because your results in the market were too good. That's on me. Now I realize we have to address it. Listen, I want you to succeed. You are a talented executive," Ken said. "But you need to change how people view you, or it will be hard for you to continue being successful inside our company."

All of this had come as a shock, and Kimberly had walked out of Ken's office feeling numb.

The more she thought about it riding home on the train now, however, Kimberly felt relieved to get these issues on the table. She had been puzzled by her colleagues' recent reactions to her success.

She had noticed that people who used to be in her corner now took potshots at her in meetings. Word got around that some were talking about her behind her back.

*Is it jealousy?* she had wondered. *I work incredibly long hours and give my heart and soul to this place. Why isn't it enough?*

However, with a twinge of guilt, Kimberly had to admit that her family was beginning to be affected by her choices too.

"Mommy, we never see you anymore," her children complained. "You're always working, even when you're home."

That had hurt, because it was true.

Her husband, Robert, often echoed the children's sentiment, trying to hide his irritation without much success.

Up until now, Kimberly had tried to adapt to all this by accelerating her Wonder Woman routine. She worked even *longer* hours, then rushed home to make dinner, help the kids with their homework, and get them to bed. To work on her relationship with Robert, Kimberly carved out an hour to watch TV with him, but she still had more to do. She might stay up late to make cupcakes for a kid's birthday party, for example, or try in vain to keep up with her friends on Facebook. Throughout it all, she was trying to respond to work emails and texts.

*The more I try to be all things for all people, the more I end up pleasing no one, including myself,* Kimberly thought. *I hate how I feel. I'm physically and emotionally spent. Ken's right. Something has to change. But what?*

Luckily, Ken recognized something many leaders miss when asking people to change. It's not enough to tell people to change. You need to provide them the tools for change too.

Therefore, after providing Kimberly feedback, Ken had given her the business card of an executive coach named Jeff.

*It's not enough to tell people to change. You need to provide them the tools for change too.*

"Jeff knows our company, Kimberly, and he has successfully worked with many of our executives before. He can help you take an objective look at all this and plot a course of action," Ken shared. "I encourage you to reach out to him."

Kimberly did reach out to Jeff and they met twice over the next few weeks. Through their conversations, Kimberly concluded that her primary problem was believing she needed to make everyone else happy.

"That must be quite a heavy burden to drag around," Jeff said.

"It is," Kimberly admitted. "When I'm at work, I feel guilty for not being at home. When I'm at home, I feel guilty for not being at work. No matter how much I do, it never feels like enough.

"But what can do I do about it?" she asked. "I can't change who I am, can I?"

"No," Jeff said. "And that's not the goal. **The goal is not to change who you are, but to change what you do so that you get better results.** And that begins with changing how you think."

As they talked about it some more, Kimberly came to realize she could not control what others felt and did. Eventually, she came up with a four-point plan she labeled "I Can Only Control Myself." She shared her plan with Jeff:

1. At work, I will help people solve problems but not solve them myself.

2. At home, I will draw clear boundaries. When I'm with family, I'll be with family. No more answering email while watching TV or having my computer out in the living room when the kids are around. Family comes first. And if, after the kids go to bed, I want to work, I'll work.

3. I will reinstate date night with Robert. At least twice a month we will go out without the kids, and I will ask him to schedule a weekend away for us occasionally too.

4. I will start exercising again and get in shape. If I'm run-down, I'm no good to anybody.

Jeff applauded Kimberly for her plan and then made a critical suggestion.

"I encourage you to share your plan for change with the people who will be impacted by it, Kimberly. Let them know what you will be changing and why," he said.

"Why? Isn't it enough that I change?" Kimberly asked.

Jeff explained that once people have their minds made up about someone, they often see what they expect. Even if you change, they probably won't notice. And he explained that if you change without letting people know why, they may fill in the blanks with negatives.

"For example, Kimberly, if you suddenly stop trying to solve people's problems at work and they don't know why, they may think you no longer care. So whenever you change, always let people know what you are doing and why. And even if you fall short in your attempts occasionally, they will be more likely to give you credit for trying.

"And finally," he added, "when you make your intention to change public, people will be more likely to hold you accountable and that can be helpful too."

Kimberly did what Jeff suggested. She met with people at work and shared why and how she was planning to change. She did the same at home with Robert too.

Kimberly noticed that just sharing her intention to change began to change some people's perceptions of her. They appreciated feeling heard. It demonstrated to them that she cared.

Kimberly made shifts on her Roadmap to support her goal of taking better care of herself too. She began to think, *Whatever I don't finish at the end of the day will still be there tomorrow. I can't get to everything, and I'm not going to kill myself trying.*

Plus, she adopted an All or Something Roadmap toward fitness too. If she couldn't make it to the gym, she would at least take the stairs at work or walk the parking lot while making phone calls.

Over time, these small changes began to have a big effect on Kimberly's results. Not having to please everyone made her more pleasing to be around.

She was more engaged with people and less stressed out. She felt more at peace. She became more effective.

Best of all, many people noticed and appreciated her efforts to change. Just as Jeff predicted, when she occasionally reverted to old habits, they gave her credit for trying.

And, as is often the case, some of Kimberly's colleagues refused to see her in a new light, no matter what she did.

"I've learned you can't please everybody!" she said to Jeff, smiling.

By changing herself, Kimberly got her relationships at work and home back on track. Most of her coworkers were willing to change their beliefs and attitudes toward her when they saw she was willing to change herself. Robert and the kids were glad to have a more engaged, rested mom at home too.

When Carson-Co's sale finally went through, Kimberly was an executive the new owners were eager to engage.

DIG A LITTLE DEEPER:
## Changing Behavior Takes Time

Changing relationships by changing yourself takes time, just as growing a garden does. You have to plant the seeds and nurture them before you can reap the harvest.

Changing your behavior requires patience, trial, and error. Sometimes you will get the new behavior right, but sometimes you'll slip back into old patterns. If you continue to change your beliefs and behaviors, both will become more ingrained over time.

Others' beliefs and attitudes toward you will gradually change too.

### Change in Real Life: Get Curious Before You Get Furious

I once had a client named Thelma. Her boss told her that she didn't listen well.

"It really makes me mad," she said. "He doesn't really know me. We don't work together in the same office, and the people I work with every day think I listen very well."

"So, how are you going to respond to your boss's feedback?" I asked.

Thelma said, "I'm going to go back and tell him that he is wrong, that I do listen well according to the people who know me best."

"Let me see if I have this right. Your boss has told you that he does not think you listen well and your strategy for handling that is to go back and tell him that he is wrong, you really do listen well?" I asked.

"Y yes," she said haltingly, as she began to catch on.

"What's the likelihood that your strategy is going to change his mind?" I asked.

"Uh, not very good," Thelma admitted sheepishly.

"Whether you listen well or not, as long as your boss believes you don't, you probably have a problem," I suggested.

"True," Thelma admitted. "How can I get him to change his mind?"

"You can't," I offered. "Only he can do that. But you can influence what he thinks by changing how you act."

"What do you mean?" Thelma asked.

"What if you got curious before you got furious?" I asked. "There must be a reason your boss thinks what he does. Instead of lashing out in anger, what if you got curious about that reason and tried to find out what it was?"

After we discussed it for a while, Thelma decided to try this tactic.

"I guess I can tell my boss that I heard he does not think that I listen well. I can ask what I do that gives him that impression. Then, I can ask how I can change that impression."

"I think you are on to something," I encouraged her.

Coming at someone in anger rarely changes how they think. Listening and seeking to understand them just might.

### Change in Real Life: What to Do When You're Not Willing to Change

John, another coaching client of mine, got feedback from his team at work that he pushed them too hard and held them to unrealistic standards.

"I am not willing to lower my standards, Gary. How can I respond to their feedback without compromising what I believe?" he asked.

"If someone wants you to do something that you are not willing to do," I replied, "the principle remains the same. Let them know that you heard them, but you don't intend to change as they wish, and tell them why. Perhaps you can negotiate from there to find a middle ground that works better for you both."

After considering this, John went back to his team. He told them that he understood that they didn't want him to push them so hard, but that he wanted them to understand he pushed them only because he wanted them to achieve their goals.

"I see potential in you that you may not see and I want to help you realize it," John said, "But maybe there is a way to do this that works better for us. Let's talk about it."

They took it from there. John and his team brainstormed a solution that everyone could live with. John acknowledged their concerns without lowering his standards and his team felt better knowing that he was listening to them.

## Knowing When to Change

Just because someone wants you to change does not mean you have to. You are the author of your life story. Consider your relationship with the person providing the feedback before changing. The more important they are to you, the more seriously you should consider their concerns.

For example, let's say my neighbor thinks I'm inconsiderate. That's very different than my wife thinking the same thing. I may or may not respond to my neighbor's feedback, but I better respond to my wife's!

Ultimately, you decide when and who you will change for, and when you won't. Let the importance of the relationship be your guide.

## QUESTIONS AND TIPS
## FOR APPLICATION

Kimberly's story illustrates some ways you could improve your relationships. Consider someone you'd like to build a better relationship with and ask—

- What do they likely believe about me right now?

_____

_____

_____

_____

- How might they be filling in the blanks about me without any evidence?

_____

_____

_____

_____

- What do I believe about them right now?

_____

_____

_____

_____

- How have I been filling in the blanks about them without any evidence?

_____

_____

_____

_____

- What might happen if I talked to them to better our mutual understanding and to fill in the blanks about each other with facts, not conjecture? How might I approach them to start such a conversation?

_____

_____

_____

_____

- If I don't know how to initiate this conversation, whom might I go to for guidance? At work, are there coaches, colleagues, or resources from HR I could consult? At home, is there a trusted friend or family member I could bounce ideas off of? The resources I will use to prepare for a difficult conversation are—

_____

_____

_____

_____

- What's one thing that I can change today for a better relationship with someone who matters to me?

_____

_____

_____

_____

## CHANGE RELATIONSHIPS BY CHANGING YOURSELF

- Changing your relationships begins by changing yourself.

- The goal is not to change who you are, but to change what you do.

- Let people know what you are going to change and why; otherwise, they may not notice it when you do.

- People tend to fill in the blanks with negatives when they don't have evidence. Fill in the blanks for them.

- Just because someone wants you to change does not mean you have to. You are the author of your life story.

*Three*

# Make a ToWho List

AS HE WEAVED HIS way through traffic, Brandon was deep in thought about his friend, Justin. They had worked side by side on the same team for eleven years before the announcement of Carson-Co's sale and the start of layoffs several weeks ago. Since then, Brandon and some others had reached out to Justin repeatedly, but they had not heard anything back.

Brandon and several of his colleagues were making good use of the outplacement services Carson-Co provided. After a few days of mutual mourning immediately following the layoffs, many of them had started looking ahead. They decided their new job was finding a job, and they proceeded accordingly.

Working with the counselors, they began to reflect on their skills and interests more deeply. They started to see how this change might ultimately become an opportunity for them to branch out and try something new. A few people even decided to pair up and start new businesses together. It was a scary but exciting time.

They often got together for impromptu socials after a day of networking and searching for jobs. Brandon noticed how this mutual bonding over their situation had affected their relationships. He saw old relationships being strengthened and new relationships taking hold. They looked forward to the camaraderie and light banter each day.

Brandon and his Carson-Co colleagues felt like they were in this change boat together, and this made the burden easier.

As the walls between them began to come down even more, they were generous about sharing networks and contacts with one another. When someone in the group found a new job, everyone was happy to raise a toast.

But of course, Justin never experienced any of this. He had never shown up.

Brandon received a call from Justin's wife, Donna, a week ago. She asked if they might get together for coffee sometime soon. She didn't provide details, but Brandon picked up that she was concerned about Justin.

"After all, you're his best friend," Donna had said.

That had taken Brandon by surprise.

*We're friendly enough,* Brandon had thought, *but I'm not sure I'd describe him as my best friend. I'm surprised he sees me that way. I wonder how many friends he actually has?*

Nevertheless, Brandon was glad Donna reached out. The two families had grown friendly. Brandon and Justin had coached their kids' soccer team together. The experience had allowed Bandon to see a part of Justin most did not get to see at work—a more fun-loving and lighthearted side.

At his best, Justin was a great father and it was fun to watch him interact with his kids.

Brandon continued to reflect as he neared the coffee shop. *Justin never let others at work really get to know him,* he thought. *I know he can be a bit of a hothead and he is set in his ways, but he's not a bad guy. It's a shame most of them never got a chance to see that.*

It was as if Justin had worn a mask at work, Brandon decided. He only let people see what he wanted them to see.

"I don't go to work to make friends," Justin had once shared.

*Mission accomplished,* Brandon thought grimly.

Without any evidence otherwise, many of Justin's coworkers had filled in the blanks with negatives. Some decided he was arrogant. Others experienced him as just plain unfriendly.

*I probably would have thought some of that too, if I hadn't known him outside of work,* Brandon thought. *He seems like two different people: a buttoned-down guy at work and a more relaxed family guy at home. It's too bad he never learned to blend the professional and personal sides of himself better.*

Brandon parked in front of the coffee shop and walked in. Donna was waiting for him.

"Thanks for agreeing to meet with me," she said as they hugged. "I didn't know where else to turn."

"Of course," Brandon replied. "You know I am here for you guys."

They grabbed their coffees and found a quiet table.

"What's going on?" Brandon asked as they settled in. "How's Justin doing?"

Donna's eyes welled with tears. "I'm worried about Justin. Ever since he was let go, he seems like a different person."

"How so?" Brandon asked.

Donna took out a tissue and dabbed at her eyes.

"I don't know. He just seems so, so angry all the time," she continued. "The littlest things seem to set him off. We have to walk on eggshells around him. He was never really like that before."

Donna paused. Brandon waited patiently.

"It's just that, well, everything seems to irritate him. Or nothing ever seems to be right," she continued.

"I don't even know what I'm trying to say," Donna said, exasperated. "I guess it's like ever since he got let go and couldn't find another job, he's gone into a shell. I try to talk to him about it, but we always end up in an argument. He won't let me in."

That resonated with the Justin Brandon knew from work.

Brandon reflected for a moment, and then said, "He hasn't reached out to me or anyone else in our group that I know of. Does he have other friends or family he goes to for support?"

"No," Donna said. "He spends most of his time alone, and the guys he does hang out with occasionally are as angry as he is. It's like they feed off of one another."

As they continued to talk, Brandon became aware of just how isolated his friend had become. *If only he had come to outplacement with the rest of us,* Brandon thought. *Maybe we could have helped him and things would be different.*

It was too late for that now.

Late afternoon slipped into evening; it was time to go.

"I'm afraid I have not been much help," Brandon said as they got up to leave.

"Oh, no," Donna reassured him, grasping his hand and looking him in the eye. "This has been very helpful. Sometimes just sharing thoughts out loud with someone who cares is enough. I definitely feel better than when I walked in, that's for sure."

"Well, then, I'm happy about that," Brandon said.

They said their goodbyes and Brandon went to pay the bill.

------

## DIG A LITTLE DEEPER:
## It's Important to Build Relationships Before Change Hits

Change is hard and having to go through it alone makes change even harder. Justin was stuck and had no one to turn to, in part because he had never built and sustained close relationships.

A ToWho List will help you avoid a similar fate. The ToWho List helps you sustain the relationships you will need when change disrupts your life.

## What is a ToWho List?

Many of us start our day by asking, "What do I need to do?" Our answers become our version of a to-do list.

Another question we might ask is, *"Whom do I want to connect with?"* Our answer to this question becomes our ToWho List.

The ToWho List contains people you don't have a specific reason to connect with right now, but who are important to you nevertheless. These people could be a client you completed a project for several months ago but are not working with currently. Or an interesting person you met at a conference last week or even a former colleague you were once close to who now works halfway around the world.

*Our ToWho List is a running record of all the people we want to sustain relationships with.*

Our ToWho List may include personal connections too. Perhaps it's family you haven't connected with in a while, sometimes even those you live with. Remember Kimberly in chapter two? Robert and the kids were feeling disconnected from her because of her work style. Working with her executive coach, Jeff, Kimberly got them back to the top of her ToWho List (and herself too).

The people on your ToWho List may be close friends you have lost touch with too.

Relationships are vital to personal happiness and professional success. Several studies have suggested a strong social network supports health and longevity. Many of us don't maintain important relationships as well as we'd like. The reasons are varied, but often it boils down to this: We get so busy doing things we don't leave time for connecting.

Items on a to-do list are transactional. People on a ToWho List are relational. The ToWho List is a process for staying connected to those who matter most.

## Our To-Do Lists Trumps Our ToWho Lists

ToWhoing someone lets them know you care about them. You can ToWho someone with small actions like checking to see how a colleague's dad is doing after surgery or sending a client an interesting article they might enjoy or even just picking up the phone to say hi.

ToWho relationships act like shock absorbers. They help us absorb the pain change sometimes creates. Without them, the change journey would be a bumpier ride.

You can't rely on relationships you never built.

*Change in Real Life: The Danger of*
*Letting Relationships Lapse*

As the psychology intern during graduate school, my job was to provide emotional support for inpatients at the physical rehab unit. One of my patients was an older, distinguished-looking gentleman whose arm had been permanently paralyzed by a stroke.

47

I visited him every day for two weeks, but he never said a word. In fact, he wouldn't even look at me. I tried everything I could think of to engage this gentleman, but nothing clicked. Until one day I said, "Sir, you have been in here for a few weeks, but I don't think I have ever seen any visitors in with you. Don't you have any family in this area?"

He turned toward me for the first time, but still he said nothing. I noticed a tear trickle down his cheek. Finally, he spoke. His voice was deep and deliberate.

"Son, I have twelve family members who live within three blocks of this hospital. None of them have visited me and none of them will. I can't blame them . . ."

I asked why.

He replied, "Before my stroke, I was one of the few in my family who had a decent job. If my family came to see me, I figured it was only for my money. I kept them away. I didn't need them, and I didn't want to have anything to do with them."

He paused again and added softly, "And now, they don't want to have anything to do with me."

Sadness echoed off the hospital room walls. I didn't know what to say. Finally, I offered feebly, "Well, at least you have your job, sir. Will you be able to return to that after you get out of the hospital?"

"Son," he said, the irony dripping from his voice, "I moved pianos."

This gentleman had not been there for his family. They were not there for him now, when he needed them most.

You must build relationships before change hits; afterward it may be too late.

*Change in Real Life: Relationships as Shock Absorbers*

Jillian was a coaching client of mine who built great relationships with her team. She got to know them as people, not just employees. She inquired about their families. She cared about their careers. She was a boss and mentor rolled into one.

Jillian was there for her team and when change hit for her, they were there for Jillian too. One year, a perfect storm of problems at home sent Jillian into an emotional tailspin. For months she struggled to find the energy needed to function her best at work. Yet, six months into the year, her results at work had never been better.

How did she do it? She didn't. They did. When Jillian's team saw her struggling, they jumped into the breach. They worked longer hours. They took extra meetings. They did whatever was needed to get the job done.

Nobody told them to do it. They stepped up because they wanted to, not because they had to. Jillian had been there for them. When she needed them, they were determined to be there for her too.

## How to Make Your ToWho List

A ToWho List is invaluable because it helps you sustain important relationships. It's easy to make and doesn't take much time.

## BEGIN BY CONSIDERING THE FOLLOWING THREE QUESTIONS:

1. Who is someone you've been meaning to get in touch with but you never seem to get around to it? (This is the person who pops in your mind from time to time and you think, *"Oh, I have to remember to reach out to so-and-so."*)

2. What friend or colleague have you lost contact with? (This is a person who you have lost touch with, and you feel it would be nice to reconnect with them.)

3. Whom do you know at work or home that could use an emotional boost or pick-me-up right about now?

Consider your answers to these questions. Write them down. Congratulations! You've just created your first ToWho List.

Many people already have a hodgepodge version of this list. They add getting in touch with someone to their to-do list, or they put sticky notes on their cubicle walls. Some even scribble names on the back of a napkin when the spirit moves. But it is easy for our ToWhos to get lost in our to-dos using these methods.

I suggest making a ToWho List that is separate from any other list.[2]

---

[2] If you prefer to use technology and have an iPhone, check out the free ToWho app for iPhone by searching for "ToWho" (one word) in the App Store.

## A SEPARATE TOWHO LIST HAS THREE PRIMARY BENEFITS:

1. It causes you to think of relationships that matter most.

2. It puts your focus on connecting with people versus transacting with them.

3. It helps you escape your problems by focusing on how you may help others with theirs.

So consider making ToWho a habit. Perhaps you can set aside a regular time of the day or week to review, edit, and act on your list. Soon ToWhoing will become a part of your normal routine.

## Making Your ToWho List a Habit

The most common objection to maintaining relationships I hear is, "*Gary, I just don't have the time.*"

Do you have three minutes to spare every day or two? If so, try the *Three-Minute Solution* outlined below. (If you don't have three minutes to spare, you may have some time management issues we need to address!)

Don't let your starting place on the Roadmap be that you *don't have time to ToWho.* Instead, change your initial thought to, "*I can't afford to not connect with those who matter most.*"

As we saw in chapter two, relationships will grow when they are nourished. Left unattended, they may wither. Use the ToWho List to help your "relationship garden" flourish.

If you want people to be there for you in the future, you need to be there for them now.

## QUESTIONS AND TIPS FOR APPLICATION

Here is the Three-Minute Solution for keeping up with your ToWho List—

- Choose a regular time and place to keep up with your ToWho List. Set aside three minutes a day or every other day (or whenever the spirit moves) to check up with the people on your ToWho List. Establishing this time will help your ToWho List become a habit.

- The time I will set aside to ToWho will be—

_____

_____

_____

_____

- Reach out to folks on your list during your ToWho time. Send a quick email, text, or note to let them know you are thinking of them.

- My preferred method for ToWhoing will be—

_____

_____

_____

_____

- You may not meet with the person you were planning on during a ToWho session, but you can still use ToWho time to schedule an in-person meeting later on, such as a lunch or call.

- The kinds of meetings I will set up when I ToWho will be—

_____

_____

_____

_____

- Carry your ToWho List with you. If you keep your list in a convenient place such as your iPhone, journal, or Excel spreadsheet, you can add to it when you think of someone you want to stay in touch with.

- I will set up my ToWho List on—

_____

_____

_____

_____

- Encourage your colleagues to ToWho and grow your collective network. Imagine the connections you can make when everyone has a ToWho List!

- The people at work I will encourage to ToWho are—

_____

_____

_____

_____

- Use your ToWho List to make a personal connection, and a professional connection will follow. People like doing business with people they know and trust.

- The people I would like to build a deeper personal connection with at work are—

_____

_____

_____

_____

## CREATE A TOWHO LIST

- If you want people to be there for you in the future, you need to be there for them now.

- You can't rely on relationships you never had.

- Take three minutes a day to make keeping up with your ToWho List a habit.

- Who will you ToWho today?

## PART TWO

# Managing Yourself
# Through Change

*Four*

# Adapt First and Fast

KEN'S FOOTSTEPS ECHOED OFF the walls as he walked down the corridor. He had just finished a difficult meeting. As Carson-Co's executive vice president of operations, he just had to tell some of its employees they were being let go as a result of the company's sale.

Ken's thoughts and feelings tumbled together as he walked back to his office. He replayed the message he had just shared in the meeting.

*"Our industry is going through a wave of consolidation. The cuts weren't due to individual performance as much as a need to cut expenses due to duplicate services."*

He wondered if the employees who had lost their jobs would understand that it was simply a business decision.

His gut didn't buy it. That guy who got up and walked out in the middle of the meeting clearly didn't buy it, either.

*Wow. How angry did he look?* Ken thought.

A twenty-two-year employee named Justin. Senior engineer. Solid performer.

*Well, Justin, we offered you a very good severance package and help with outplacement. What else do you want us to do?*

Somewhere deep in the back of his mind, Ken knew the answer. There wasn't anything else he or the others in senior leadership could do now.

*We should have seen change coming! We should have adapted sooner. How did we let this happen?*

Ken turned the problem over in his mind. For years, Carson-Co had enjoyed steady, if unspectacular, results. True, market share had begun to slowly erode over the last few years, but *they had convinced themselves it was just the normal market cycle.*

Ken thought the company culture was strong but insular. The board was stocked mostly with company insiders. Long-time employees knew each other well. Almost too well.

*We're hesitant to challenge one another. We avoid conflict. We value harmony over having the tough conversation.*

*That worked okay as long as the industry was stagnant,* he thought. *When things began to change, we missed it, partly because we were afraid to challenge our old ways of thinking and doing things.*

They had been slow to innovate. They hadn't invested enough in new technology. Their management philosophy had been "Why change and make risky investments when nothing is obviously broken?"

Some of their more talented young people could read the tea leaves and quit. They preferred a forward-looking organization to one focused on clinging to the past.

Longtime but mediocre performers who preferred the status quo stayed on. *We closed our eyes to that trend too*, Ken thought, shaking his head at what seemed so obvious in hindsight.

Lacking sufficient input from outside the company walls, company leadership had become tone-deaf. Subtle shifts in consumer demands went unnoticed. The impact of technological advances was too quickly dismissed.

Carson-Co's leaders had thought these trends were just fads. Rather than taking a risk, they stuck to what had always worked for them.

Reaching his office, Ken closed the door, sat down, and slowly rocked back and forth in his chair. He realized they had been complacent. Arrogant, too. Change was happening, but they never saw it coming because they really didn't want to.

Because nothing was obviously broken, Carson-Co's leaders saw nothing to fix.

*Now that it's clear something is broken, it's too late*, Ken thought. *Our competitor saw an opening and pounced. We have no one to blame but ourselves.*

Soon, Carson-Co as he knew it, with its proud tradition and heritage, would be no more. Ken closed his eyes and tried to push such thoughts from his mind. But the image of Justin angrily stomping out of the meeting remained seared in his consciousness.

---

## DIG A LITTLE DEEPER:
# Nothing Fails Like Success

I like to ask my keynote audiences, "How many of you used to rent movies from Blockbuster?"

Nearly everyone raises their hand. Then, I ask how many *still* rent movies from Blockbuster? Wry laughter sweeps the crowd. Maybe one hand goes up.

In 2004, Blockbuster had over 9,000 stores and 60,000 employees. They were the behemoth in the movie rental industry. In 2010, they declared bankruptcy. What happened? How do you go from top of the heap to nearly extinct in *six short years?*

The answer? Blockbuster's failure to adapt fast enough to an innovative competitor: Netflix.

Reed Hastings founded Netflix when he saw a market opportunity in the late 1990s. Using the emerging technology of the Internet, customers could pay a monthly subscription fee with no late charges. Rather than stopping by a store, customers could go to a website and select movies to be mailed directly to their house.

The concept was simple, but it wasn't perfect. There was no ability to spontaneously pick up a movie on your way home from work. There was no opportunity to browse through titles on the shelf. Plus, Blockbuster had a huge customer base compared to a relatively small one for Netflix.

In 2000, Hastings approached Blockbuster about partnering up. Blockbuster declined. I can't say why, but it's not a stretch to conclude they may have fallen prey to complacency and arrogance. It's easy to do.

The reason? **Nothing fails like success.**

It's easy to get people to buy in to change when disaster looms on the doorstep. It is harder to do when everyone feels comfortable where they are.

Let's use the Roadmap to explore how this can happen to otherwise smart executives like Ken and his colleagues in the C-suite at Carson-Co, and, perhaps, to smart executives in your company too.

The leadership Roadmap before Carson-Co was acquired looked something like this:

- *Thinking:* We're doing well enough; change is risky; let's stay the course.

- *Feelings:* Safety and comfort

- *Behavior:* Complacency and doing what they've always done

- *Results:* Short-term success and long-term failure

If you're standing still, like Carson-Co did, your competitors are not.


## The Four Factors Driving Change Globally

There are four factors that drive change for businesses:

- Government regulations

- Technology

- Industry consolidation

- Globalization

Everyone is handed these four pieces to the puzzle of change. Organizations that win put them together faster and better than their competition. Because these factors are constantly changing the market landscape, what worked yesterday most likely won't work tomorrow.

*Going through change is not a market differentiator. Adapting to change faster and better than your competition can be.*

Going through change is not a market differentiator. Adapting to change faster and better than your competition can be.

Let me rephrase that slightly: You *must* adapt to change faster and better than your competition if you want to stay in the game. If you're not adapting, you're falling behind. And catching up is hard.

### Change in Real Life: You're Either Leading the Way or Losing Your Way

A few years ago the taxicab industry was panicking due to a new competitor, Uber. The taxi industry had been slow to innovate, and then Uber introduced new technology that radically disrupted the market. The taxicab industry has been playing technology catch-up ever since.

Or consider the mobile phone industry. When Apple released the first iPhone in 2007, some pundits said they were doomed. After all, everyone knew Blackberry, owned by Research in Motion, had that market locked up.

Just a few years later, Blackberry was hanging on by a thread. They had failed to adapt quickly enough to innovations introduced by their competitors, primarily Apple.

Now, Apple cannot afford to stand still. Samsung has a higher market share as of this writing. Apple will need strong leadership to maintain their edge in releasing innovative products that solve problems consumers did not know that they had.

And Netflix, whom we mentioned earlier, continues to try and stave off competitors like Hulu and Amazon by creating new content, technologies, and even new markets. Constant change demands strong leadership from companies and individuals looking to stay ahead of their competitors.

## Adapting First and Fast Requires Leadership

Perhaps it would be helpful to think of change and leadership as two strands of the same rope. One begets the other. In fact, if there were no change, we wouldn't need leaders. Managing to the status quo would do.

But change happens, and we need leaders to help us adapt to it. When change *needs* to happen, we need leaders to show us the way. Carson-Co and other examples cited in this chapter are cautionary tales of what can happen when leadership is lax about change.

*If there were no change, we wouldn't need leaders.*

I encourage you to hone your leadership skills, no matter your title, level, or station in life. The demand for adaptive leadership won't end anytime soon.

## Dealing with Change Fatigue

Some of my clients say, "Gary, we don't mind change, and we can see the need to adapt first and fast. But we're tired of the pace of change; we wish things would just level out for a while."

I understand. However, imagine you are in the hospital and hooked up to a heart monitor. When you look at that monitor, do you want to see a line constantly changing, up and down, up and down?

Or would you prefer a nice smooth line with no change at all?

Life is change, and change is life. We'd best get used to it.

## What if We Never Changed Personally?

So far in this chapter, we have addressed the need for adapting and changing at work. But consider for a moment: What if we never changed personally? What if we reached our mid-twenties, say, and stopped adapting and advancing? Imagine a picture of yourself back then. If you're like me, that's a bleak picture. Literally. Experience has taught me:

*"When we are through changing, we are through."*
—Bruce Barton

## Get Comfortable with Being Uncomfortable

Sometimes we avoid change because it makes us feel uncomfortable. That's understandable.

Think about it like this: If you go to the gym and get a good workout, you will feel sore the next day. That's a good thing, right? It means you are making a change in your body, which was probably your goal in the first place.

Maybe you can think about change the same way. At first, it may make you feel uncomfortable. But being a little uncomfortable now may help you advance to something better later on.

> **Get comfortable being uncomfortable.**

Leaders can help overcome this tendency to stagnate by encouraging followers to **get comfortable being uncomfortable.** In fact, the best leaders continually nudge people out of their comfort zones to help them adapt and advance.

Our world rewards those who adapt first and fast, something Ken and his colleagues at Carson-Co realized too late. To help you adapt and advance to change at work or home, consider the questions and tips below.

## QUESTIONS AND TIPS
## FOR APPLICATION

What if we gave Ken and Carson-Co a do-over?

- If they could turn back the clock a few years, how might Ken and his colleagues think differently about the change happening within their industry?

_____

_____

_____

_____

- What thoughts and feelings may have been driving their reluctance to challenge one another and avoid conflict?

_____

_____

_____

_____

- How might they change their thinking about conflict in the future to get better results?

_____

_____

_____

_____

- What new beliefs might they embrace to support a more creative and innovative culture?

_____

_____

_____

_____

Now let's take a look at your situation.

- Are there any aspects of the Carson-Co story that you see in your organization or in your life? If so, what are they?

_____

_____

_____

_____

- How might you alter your beliefs around the need to change and adapt as a result?

_____

_____

_____

_____

- How might you make yourself comfortably uncomfortable to help you grow in your career and in life?

_____

_____

_____

_____

- As a leader at work and at home, how can you make others comfortably uncomfortable to help them adapt and advance too?

_____

_____

_____

_____

- How can you apply what you've learned from the cautionary tales in this chapter to better lead your organization, family, or community, no matter your official role or title?

_____

_____

_____

_____

## ADAPT FIRST AND FAST

- What if change isn't the problem? What if change is the answer?

- The time to get most nervous is when you are the most successful.

- Leaders help people get comfortable with being uncomfortable.

- You already know what you think. Surround yourself with smart people who think differently.

- What will you do to get uncomfortable today to help you adapt and advance?

*Five*

# Let Go

AS SHE RUSHED DOWN the hall to yet another meeting, Cheryl reflected on the dizzying pace of the last few months. *All I seem to do anymore is go to meetings,* she thought. *It would be nice to have some time to do my actual job.*

Life had been a whirlwind ever since the deal for acquiring Carson-Co had been announced.

Following the initial round of layoffs, the rumor mill was running rampant. There were rumors of more layoffs and even the entire company shutting down. Of course, none of the rumors had basis in reality, but that didn't seem to matter.

*Unchecked fear can do amazing things to the way people think and act,* Cheryl thought.

Things at home were as chaotic as ever too. If anything, Edward's travel had increased and the situation at Carson-Co was absorbing even more of Cheryl's time and energy than before. Like a tuning fork, the kids seemed to vibrate at the levels of stress in the home. Right now, that fork was humming.

*At least the latest crisis with Mom passed and I didn't have to fly out there this time,* Cheryl thought, quickening her pace, fearing she would be late to her meeting. *I suppose it's only a matter of time before something happens again and I will. Poor Mom and Dad. Getting old is hard. Should I bring up the subject of them moving into a senior living facility again?*

Cheryl winced. She had gently hinted at this idea before on a phone call with her fiercely independent parents; the response had been an icy silence.

*Still, something has to give,* she thought. *I can't keep going like this indefinitely. Neither can they.*

Cheryl reached the door to the meeting room. She paused before going in and took a deep breath to collect herself.

*I have to remember to catch up with Kimberly to find out what she has been doing to take better care of herself physically,* Cheryl thought.

Kimberly had shared that she was going to be working on her physical fitness and managing her personal energy, and Cheryl had noticed the difference.

*Kimberly seems more engaged and less stressed out than she used to be,* Cheryl thought. *Whatever she's doing, it seems to be working for her. I could use some tips!*[3]

After the meeting, Cheryl had some time to walk the halls and visit informally with the folks in her department. She had regularly practiced this technique of "management by walking around" most of her career, and now it was more important than ever.

---

3   For more info on managing human energy, check out the excellent work of the Johnson & Johnson Human Performance Institute at https://www.jjhpi.com/.

Cheryl took pride in being good at the people part of her job, because she had worked at it. Although she did not consider herself a natural people person, Cheryl knew she was only as good as the people who worked for her. It was in her best interests and theirs to lead them as best she could.

Cheryl had taken all the leadership classes that Carson-Co had offered and now she was particularly glad that she did. The company's acquisition, and all it required of her, was like taking a final exam on leadership. It was time to apply what she had learned.

The best way to quash the rumor mill was to nip it in the bud, Cheryl had learned. The best way to nip it was to get out there and listen to what people were afraid of and then help them to let go of those fears.

Therefore, her starting place on the Roadmap as she walked the halls and shop floor became—

*Find out what people are thinking and feeling about the change. Don't assume people think and feel about it like you do, or should.*

Cheryl realized that senior leaders often consider changes for months, or even years, before a change is announced. They had plenty of time to get acclimated to the idea and decide if and how it happened. This wasn't the case for the employees affected by the change.

*Our employees haven't been living and breathing this change for the last several months like management has,* Cheryl thought.

*Making a major announcement where you state the company's case for change, take a few questions, and expect people to "get it" just doesn't work. You have to give people time to wrap their minds around the change. Help them get to a better starting place on their Roadmaps, so they end up in a better place.*

Cheryl's approach was to ask questions.

*"How are you feeling about things now, Sarah?" "What's the latest in the rumor mill, Cindy?" "Any questions I can answer for you, Muhammad?"*

Cheryl was careful to listen and respond to her team's answers, instead of rushing to formulate her next question. In fact, after one of her classes on leadership and listening, Cheryl had taken a marker and written in big, bold letters:

## Leaders ask more than they tell, and they listen more than they talk.

She taped this statement to the cover of her tablet as a daily reminder. She made these thoughts part of her Roadmap when she made her rounds each day. She found practicing these principles at home made her a better partner and parent, too.

Cheryl supplemented this approach with a simple yet often overlooked change leadership principle: Tell them the truth.

*Seems easy enough,* Cheryl thought.

She was amazed how many times her fellow leaders had failed to heed this critical principle over the last several weeks. Afraid of how people might respond, some of her colleagues tiptoed around the truth. They were afraid if they shared too much information people would get spooked.

Predictably, the opposite happened. People's BS detectors were engaged, and they could sense their leaders were not being fully transparent. Employees filled in the blanks with negatives. As their fears increased, their trust of leadership decreased.

Cheryl took the opposite tack. She told the truth, as she knew it. "*Be transparent*" was her mantra. *Tell them what you know and what you don't know. If you don't know something, let them know when you expect to find out.*

Of course, she employed common sense. She didn't always go into details, and there were some things she was not at liberty to discuss. She was open about sharing that fact when necessary, too.

Overall, Cheryl discovered that, contrary to Jack Nicholson's famous line in the movie *A Few Good Men*, people in fact *could* handle the truth. It was being fed an obvious company line meant to mollify them that people would not tolerate.

Before leaving her office to make her rounds, Cheryl made it a habit to take out her iPhone and glance at her ToWho List. Today it read, "*Stop by Jody's cubicle and congratulate him on the new baby.*"

As she walked and interacted with folks, Cheryl noticed that people's reactions to change generally fell into three buckets.

Roughly ten percent of the people were entrenched in the old ways and would never let go. *We tried that before and it didn't work then, and it won't work now,* was where they started and ended on the Roadmap. She avoided the seductive trap of putting all her energies into this often vocal but intransigent group.

A second group was about the same size as the first, but started with an opposite Roadmap.

This group's mind-set was that every change is rife with opportunity, including this one, and they were energized. All Cheryl had to do was point them in the right direction and they would be fine.

The third group, and by far the largest one, fell in the middle. They were open to letting go of the old, but they needed help shifting their Roadmaps to get there. They needed to be led.

Cheryl focused most of her time and energy on this middle group when she did her rounds. *If I can help the majority let go and move on, the company will move on too,* she thought.

To help them think differently about the future, Cheryl shared with them a vision of what the new organization might look like and how they might fit in.

She shared where she saw potential opportunities, and how they might start preparing themselves to take advantage of those opportunities.

"If you view this change as an opportunity, and get ready now, you'll be ready to take advantage when the time comes," she told them. "Anticipate the skills that will be needed in the new organization and start reading up on them, or start taking classes to get yourselves up to speed.

"Think about it," she added. **Who's going to do better in the long run? Those complaining about the change, or those doing something about it?**

"In the meantime, keep doing your job and serving your customers. I can guarantee you that's a value that's not going to change. And it's the best way I know to position yourself for a role in the new organization, no matter what happens."

Cheryl noticed that a few people had trouble following her advice. Some lived in the past and wished things could go back to the way they were. Others lived in the future, paralyzed by fears of what might happen next.

In either case, weighed down by these beliefs, both groups were underperforming relative to their peers who were ready to let go and move on.

*I need to keep searching for ways to help people let go of whatever is holding them down or holding them back,* Cheryl thought. *It's impossible to move on to the future when you're holding on to the past or worrying about what might happen next.*

---

### DIG A LITTLE DEEPER:
## You Can't Move On by Holding On

Some of us struggle to let go of the past. Like Justin and some of those on Cheryl's team, we hold on to old beliefs, old ways, and old practices. The world moves on, but we don't. Because, as we learned in chapter four, change makes us feel uncomfortable. So we hold on to what we know, even when it's against our best interests.

Sometimes we live in an "if only" world consumed by resentments and regrets from the past. We can be consumed by thoughts like, "If only I had gone to a different school," "If only I had accepted that other job," or "If only I had a different boss, then I could be happy."

At other times, we get stuck imagining a frightening future. We live in a scary world of "what if" scenarios. We think, "What if the stock market crashes again, and I lose my retirement savings?" or "What if I lose my job?"

Then, we react emotionally as if these scenarios have happened. Our fears can then drive behavior that creates the very outcome we sought to avoid.

For example, panic may cause us to sell retirement investments at the bottom of the market, and excessive worry may cause us to perform poorly on the job. At home, fear of rejection could cause us to be walled off in a relationship, and our partner eventually tires of our lack of vulnerability and moves on.

Whether we are consumed by resentment from the past or fears of the future, the outcome is the same: We may miss opportunities now.

It's as if we're relying on an outdated Roadmap. The environment around us has changed, but we have failed to adapt. Unless we update our Roadmap by adopting new mind-sets, we may be left behind.

*Freedom Comes from Letting Go*

## Freedom Comes from Letting Go

What if our Roadmap for change started with this thought: *Freedom comes from letting go*? Where might it lead?

### Change in Real Life: Shaquila Learns to Let Go

A few years ago, I had a friend named Shaquila who was unhappy working for her dad in the family business. She believed he did not value her contributions, ignored her ideas, and unfairly criticized her work.

Shaquila tried to adapt by moving to another part of the operation, but to no avail. There, she encountered an incompetent manager who frustrated her even more. She butted heads with this person repeatedly.

Shaquila complained, but apparently the manager was one of Dad's favorites, and her complaints fell on deaf ears. Shaquila's dissatisfaction and unhappiness grew, and she thought she knew where to lay the blame.

"I was sure Dad and the other manager were my problem, Gary. I used to think, *If only Dad would listen to me. If only that other manager would go away. If only I had my own operation to run free from their interference, then I would be happy.*"

Shaquila considered quitting, but then worried, "*What if the new job was even worse?*"

One day after a long run to clear her mind, Shaquila decided to write down everything she was thinking and feeling to see if that would help. She pulled out an old journal and began to write.

*I want a new and better life. I will let go of old thoughts and feelings that are holding me back and create new ones that serve me better.*

A few days later, Shaquila picked it up and read what she wrote. Calmer now and with a clearer eye, she was amazed by what she saw.

"I blamed my problems on everyone *but* me!" she said. "Dad was the problem, not me. The other manager was the problem, not me. Circumstances beyond my control were the problem. Nothing was ever my fault. I had let myself become a victim. I *realized I would never get ahead thinking like that.*

"I decided to start thinking and acting more positively. I wrote my new thoughts down:

*I want a new and better life. I will let go of old thoughts and feelings that are holding me back and create new ones that serve me better.*

Ultimately, these thoughts led Shaquila to the path of forgiveness.

"How so?" I asked her. "What does forgiveness have to do with letting go?"

Shaquila answered by sharing this Nelson Mandela quote with me:

> *"As I walked out the door toward the gate*
> *that would lead to my freedom,*
> *I knew if I didn't leave my bitterness and*
> *hatred behind, I'd still be in prison."*

"Gary," Shaquila said, "This quote really resonated with me. I realized that my prison was the belief that everyone else was responsible for my happiness, not me. As long as I believed that, I would never be happy."

Shaquila realized another thing. "The only one who suffers when I carry a grudge is me," she said.

Shaquila decided to switch the starting place on her Roadmap. She wrote it down in her journal:

> No one is responsible for my happiness but me.
> Forgiveness is the key to my freedom. When others have wronged me, I will forgive them.
> I refuse to carry the burden of resentment.

Ever since, things have gotten much better.

"My relationships with Dad and the other manager have improved, and I am happier and more effective at work. I let it all go," Shaquila reported.

Shaquila's story is a powerful one. It highlights that, often, the path to letting go begins with forgiveness. Letting go is a three-step process:

1. It begins by deciding you want a better outcome in your life.

2. It continues with letting go of blaming others, or yourself, for your current circumstance.

3. It ends with creating new thoughts and behaviors, to create new results.

Following are some ideas to help you let go of whatever is holding you down or holding you back.

## QUESTIONS AND TIPS FOR APPLICATION

Think about a change you are struggling with, at work or in life, and ask—

- Am I hanging on to thoughts, feelings, or behaviors regarding this change that are only holding me down or holding me back?

_____

_____

_____

_____

- Am I getting anything as a result?

_____

_____

_____

_____

- Am I blaming others for my problems? If so, who? What is that getting me?

_____

_____

_____

_____

- Am I blaming myself or beating myself up? If so, where is that getting me?

_____

_____

_____

_____

- Is there anyone I want to forgive, perhaps even myself? The people I will forgive are—

_____

_____

_____

_____

- If you are holding on to a fearful future that's holding you back, you might ask—

_____

_____

_____

_____

- What is going on right here and now? Is there anything that is going to immediately cause me physical harm? If not, exactly what am I afraid of?

_____

_____

_____

_____

- Instead of worrying about the future, what can I do to address my concerns now? For example, if I am worried about losing my job, what can I do to prepare for the next one? If I am worried about future finances, how can I make contingency plans now?

_____

_____

_____

_____

## LET GO

- Holding on only holds you back.

- Letting go means not blaming others for your problems. Or yourself.

- Letting go means accepting that life will never be perfect and neither will you. That's okay.

- Forgiveness is the key to letting go of resentments from the past.

- Planning and acting on your plan is the key to letting go of fears about the future.

*Six*

# Latch On

*KIMBERLY WILL BE PERFECT for this role,* Ken thought.

Ever since her talks with Jeff, the young executive had been working hard to be a good colleague within Carson-Co's new company, not just a superstar out in the market.

*Giving her a significant role on the Culture Transition Team is a perfect next step in her development,* Ken concluded.

At first, Kimberly was surprised by the assignment. It involved assessing and integrating the cultures of the two combining companies. Dealing with the softer side of business had not exactly been her forte in the past. Ken explained that it was precisely because she had been working on the softer side of things that she was chosen.

"We've got plenty of people who understand the business and can crunch the numbers, Kimberly. We have some other folks who get the people side too. We need someone who gets both," he said. "Those people are much rarer and harder to find. You should feel flattered."

Kimberly wasn't quite sure flattered was the word. She was glad Ken and the other C-suite execs had noticed her efforts to change. Although the new assignment meant more hours on top of her already heavy schedule, she wasn't too worried about that either. Her focus on managing her energy should continue to pay dividends there.

In fact, colleagues had noticed her working on that just as she said she would, and they started coming to her for advice on how they could too.

As Kimberly began to research culture and company integrations, she was not too surprised at what she learned. Often, misaligned cultures and values were cited as contributing factors when deals did not pan out as well as expected. The logical, business case for the deals had been solid, but the cultures and values of the combining companies had clashed.

For example, she read about a failed venture where one company valued innovation and risk taking, while their merger partner was considerably more conservative and risk averse. In another example, one company valued robust discussion and open conflict, while their merger partner preferred camaraderie and consensus to conflict.

*Left unchecked, these differences in values could become the poison that kills an otherwise beautiful marriage,* Kimberly realized.

These particular examples caused her concern, as they hit too close to home.

Kimberly knew the company acquiring Carson-Co well. She had been competing with them since her first day on the job. They always seemed one step ahead of Carson-Co and their other competitors when it came to bringing innovative products and services to market.

*It's not a surprise they initiated the merger even though they are a younger company and smaller than us. It's in keeping with their high-risk culture. They do their homework and are not afraid to take high-risk chances.*

This was in stark contrast to Carson-Co's "steady as she goes" approach.

Kimberly realized that the combined company could be dead in the water if they didn't manage their culture and values right.

Kimberly and her team worked closely with their counterparts in the acquiring company. They used surveys and interviews to assess the current values and Roadmap patterns in both companies. What they found was typical in many companies that merge.

For the most part, employees in both legacy companies paid little attention to formal pronouncements. Instead, they paid much closer attention to who got plum assignments in the new combined company. They kept a tally of how many spots went to leaders and managers from their own company versus the other.

Additionally, no matter how many in management tried to sell the idea that this was a merger of equals, most employees didn't buy it. Many of them looked at it and thought, *If our leaders are out and their leaders are in, that doesn't sound too equal.*

Worse, Kimberly's team discovered, there were some managers in Carson-Co running around telling people the layoffs were over and everyone could relax.

Although it was true that no more layoffs were planned at present, common sense said the need for more layoffs might emerge as business conditions dictated. Most employees understood this, even if some in management apparently did not. Managers who repeated the line about no more layoffs were damaging their credibility.

As Kimberly and her team wrapped up their assessment, they agreed one group at Carson-Co stood out from the rest. People there seemed well informed and up-to-date on the latest happenings relative to the deal. As a result, they seemed less anxious than their peers. Most of these team members were focusing on doing their jobs, instead of worrying if they would still have one post-integration.

Intrigued, Kimberly interviewed the group's manager to find out what made them different. Turns out, it was leadership. Cheryl was happy to share her approach.

"When I took over this department things were a mess," Cheryl explained. "They had had three different managers during the previous nine months, each with a different style and approach. I came in and no one knew what to expect. Suspicion was at an all-time high, and trust at an all-time low."

"I think we have several groups about to experience something similar once the integration fully takes place, if we don't manage it right, " Kimberly said. "We have a lot of groups with low trust levels right now. How did you approach it? What did you do to fix it?"

"Well, I wouldn't say I fixed it," Cheryl replied. "It was more of a gradual process and group effort."

Cheryl explained that when she came in, the group was fractured. They needed something to bring them together. So one of the first things Cheryl and her team did was talk about what kind of group they wanted to be and how they wanted to operate together.

"We got everyone involved, not just few leaders at the top," Cheryl said. "Of course, I set the overall business direction, but I wanted them to set the values and approach of how we would get there."

Cheryl knew if she and her team didn't latch on to a common set of core values about how they wanted to interact and operate, any strategy she set would be moot.

"Any initiatives we tried would be undermined by the low-trust culture. So we needed to get that part right," Cheryl said.

"You mentioned culture and values, together," Kimberly said, glancing down at her notes. "Tell me more about that. How are the two related in your mind?"

"Well, there's lots of different ways of looking at it," Cheryl answered. "I think of culture as the way things get done around here and how we treat one another while we're doing it. Our values are part of our culture, too. In many ways they help to define it. We use them as a practical, every-day tool to help run our business too."

"How does that work, exactly?" Kimberly asked.

Cheryl explained that her group thought of values like a compass. When they had tough decisions to make and were not sure which way to turn, they used their values to point them in the right direction.

"Can you give me an example of what you mean?" Kimberly asked.

"Sure," Cheryl replied. "Last week we had a tough call to make on dealing with a sensitive customer issue. There were strong arguments on both sides on how to handle it. In our group, we resolve differences like that by going back to our values.

"We ask, 'Which alternative course of action is most in keeping with our values?' Whatever it is, that's the path we take."

Kimberly asked, "Does that make things easier for you?"

"No, not always," Cheryl admitted. "Our values always point us in the right direction, but the right direction is not always the easiest one. Sometimes it might be easier to cut corners, but our values help us stay on track and true to ourselves."

"Fascinating," Kimberly said. "Tell me, how do you keep values top of mind? How do you keep everybody on board with them? Do you print them up and hand out cards or something?"

Cheryl tried to suppress a chuckle. "I'm sorry, I don't mean to laugh, but no, it's much more ingrained than that. I mean, we have them printed up, and they are on the department website, but if people don't internalize the values, they become nothing more than words on the wall.

"Our values are real because we talk about them every day. Hardly a meeting passes without the values being mentioned as a guide to our decisions. Values are not separate from our business. They are a part of it and help to define how we operate.

"We recruit for values too," Cheryl continued. "No matter how technically skilled someone might be, or how strong our need, we'll take a pass on hiring them if their values don't mesh with ours. We've discovered that any short-term gain will turn into long-term pain if we get people in here that don't align with our values."

"Oh, I think that explains something else to me too," Kimberly said. "We've noticed that your group seems much more informed regarding the integration relative to other groups we have surveyed. Does that have something to do with your values as well?"

"I'd like to think so," Cheryl answered. "One of my personal values is openness and transparency. I have tried to practice that since the day I got here. It has been very helpful to mc as I lcad my group through this transition.

She went on to explain that she didn't have to wonder what to share and how to share it. Cheryl would tell her group what she knew and what she didn't. "I don't sugarcoat things. I try to answer their questions as honestly as I can. They appreciate that."

"Our assessment suggests that as well," Kimberly offered. "The morale in your group is second to none, from what we have seen."

"Well, I am glad to hear that," Cheryl said. "It's good to know we are on the right track."

"This has been fascinating and very helpful," Kimberly added. "Thank you so much."

Kimberly walked back to her office to debrief with her team; she reflected on what Cheryl had shared. *Whatever else we do in this cultural transition, we need to define and latch on to a common set of core values about what matters most.*

## DIG A LITTLE DEEPER:
## The Two-Minute Drill

One of the most popular segments of my keynotes on leading change is *The Two-Minute Drill*. It's a brief writing exercise designed to help people quickly get in touch with their personal values.[4] You may want to try the drill for yourself.

---

4   The drill is derived from ideas I got from the works of Stephen Covey, author of *The Seven Habits of Highly Effective People*, and Randy Pausch, author of *The Last Lecture*.

(*Note:* I always set this up as a private process. If you are reading this book with others and choose to do the drill, please do not press anyone to share their results unless they choose to.)

The exercise begins when I ask people to think about a child they love with all their heart and soul. If they don't have children, I ask them to think about a niece, nephew, or grandchild. It can be a grown child or infant.

Heck, I tell them, if you're an older character like me, it could even be a youngster on your team at work that you love as if they were a child of your own.

Next, I say, "In a moment I am going to say, 'Go.' When I say, 'Go,' you will have two minutes to write that child a letter. We are going to pretend that something has happened to you, not to the child. We are going to pretend that you will never have another opportunity to communicate with this child ever again, except for this letter that I will give you two minutes to write. No texts, calls, conversations, or emails. This is it."

*Values are the deeply personal starting place on everyone's Roadmap.*

When I say, "Go," they (and you) need to write down everything this child needs to know about life and what matters most. I recommend writing a stream of consciousness. Don't think; write. Remember, this letter is your last chance to ever communicate with this child and to let them know what life is all about.

You have two minutes. Go.

The room goes silent. Heads drop and pens or thumbs fly (if they choose to write on their smartphones or tablets). The two minutes go by fast.

"Stop!" I call out at the end. When people look up, it's not unusual to see some in the audience dabbing at tears.

*The Two-Minute Drill* is a powerful way for people to connect to their core values. It helps them experience not just the beliefs behind their values but the emotions tied to those beliefs too.

Values are the foundational mind-set for your life and how you relate with others.

So why do I have folks get in touch with their values in a talk about change? Because the one thing that change can't touch is your values. Values are timeless. They are yours. No boss, company, or change in your lifetime can alter your values, unless you choose to let them.

As we learned from Cheryl, values are a practical tool to help us cope with change too. Personally, when you are feeling overwhelmed by change and have lost your way, latch on to your values. They will act as your compass and point you in the right direction.

### *Change in Real Life: Using Values as a Compass to Get Back on Track*

One evening during the early years of growing my business, I came home for a quick dinner with the family, in between business development meetings.

As I got up to leave, my six-year-old asked, "Daddy, where are you going?"

"To a business meeting," I replied.

"You just got home!" he sighed.

I tried to reassure my son, "I'll be back in a few hours."

"But I'll be asleep!"

"I'll give you a kiss when I get in," I told him.

"Wait a minute!" he said, running of the room. He came back and handed me his picture.

"What's this?" I asked.

"Here!" he said in his most dramatic, Hollywood-like voice. "Take this to remember me by!"

*Give me a break,* I thought. *I'm only going to be gone for a few hours!*

As I drove to my meeting, I reflected on my son's message. I realized he was communicating, in his own unique way, that I was not as present as he had needed me to be. He was right. I had been so busy building my business that I had begun to neglect my home.

*His mother and sister likely need more from me too,* I thought as I drove.

I considered my values, which I had clearly defined when I started my business. *First, take care of family. Second, take care of clients.*

My son's feedback helped me realize my behavior had slipped. I had it reversed. Business development was trumping family. That's not the way I had drawn it up.

That weekend I was scheduled to take yet another out of town sales trip. I pulled out my values compass and thought things through. Business was going well. I was covering the bills. The trip was not vital.

That weekend I stayed home and reconnected with my family instead. Values, and some well-timed feedback from my son, helped get me back on track.

### Change in Real Life: How Values Can Act Like Radar Too

An executive approached me after one of my talks. He was disillusioned; he worked for a company known for their strong core values.

He said, "Gary, our company was built on values that I'm proud of and live by. But recently some people in my group are acting so counter to our values I took my office poster of them down. We're hypocrites. Right now we are not living by what we say we believe."

"I hear you," I said. "I understand your frustration. But is it possible that you are abandoning your values just when you need them most?"

He looked at me quizzically.

"Nobody is perfect," I continued. "We slip up from time to time. We can slide off course despite our best intentions. When we do, that's where our values show their worth. Because values, like radar, can let us know we have drifted."

"Tell me more," he said.

"Let's say you're flying a plane," I said. "You set a course for your destination, but rarely is it a straight-line journey. Storms, wind, air traffic, all kinds of things may knock you off course along the way. When you drift off course, your radar will alert you. When it does, will you get frustrated and turn the radar off? Or will you use it to get back on track?"

"Well, of course the latter," he said.

"Good! Values work the same way," I said. "Right now your values at work are alerting you that your group is off course. Rather than rejecting your values now, it would seem you need them more than ever to help get your group get back on track."

"I hear what you're saying," he said. "And my values would say I need to speak up to help us get back on track. Not everyone is going to want to hear what I have to say. Some will want to shoot the messenger, and that messenger would be me!"

"Agreed," I said. "That's why it takes courage to follow our values sometimes. Like we learned earlier, values will always point us in the right direction, not necessarily the easiest direction. It sounds like your colleagues need you to speak up."

I sometimes think of values as the backbone of courage. The test of values is whether you use them when you need them most.

*You know corporate values are real when you use them every day to make decisions.*

## How Do You Know When Values Are Real?

Unfortunately, for many organizations, values are nothing more than words on the wall, remnants from decisions made at some distant management offsite.

To find out if your corporate values are real, try asking random employees what the organization's values are. Beware if they answer something like, "Uh, I think it has something to do with customer service, or something about people being our most important asset? Is that right?"

These answers show that your values aren't real. If employees can quickly and easily state what the values are, they *may* be real. You know corporate values are real when you use them every day to make decisions.

### CHANGE IN REAL LIFE:
## Using Values to Drive Business Results

My client Jose was appointed the leader of a dysfunctional group. He had hundreds of sales executives geographically dispersed around the globe who embodied an anti-team: They did not cooperate and, instead of collaborating, competed with each other. It was every man and woman for themselves. Not surprisingly, the group's financial results were not stellar.

Jose was determined to change the business by changing the culture. Values became his primary tool.

Jose and his team defined four fundamental values: We are one unified group. We exist to serve our customers. We act with integrity. We treat each other as we want to be treated.

At first, Jose's team's new values felt like words on the wall. Over time, however, they helped transform his organization. They regularly used the values to make decisions, discussing them in every meeting like, "Well, because we act with integrity, the way to go on this would be . . ."

Gradually, other leaders in the organization began to follow suit. The values became a part of their everyday lexicon and operating model.

To help drive the values throughout the organization, Jose and a team of consultants designed a leadership development program that behaviorally defined and reinforced the values.

Jose and his team recognized that behavior change is a gradual process, so they took their time. For example, rather than put everyone through the leadership program at once, they did groups of thirty or so every three or four months.

This way, every few months, a new turbocharged group of sales folks, infused with a new burst of energy, reinforced the values throughout the organization.

Gradually, the new values-based culture took root for Jose's team. Teamwork improved and collaboration increased. Revenue and profitability soared.

Years later, many executives pointed to that transformative period in the organization as one of the most rewarding of their careers.

## How Values Can Help Companies Endure

Many well-known, successful companies use values as their compass. For example, when Apple's CEO Tim Cook was interviewed by Rick Tetzeli in the March 2015 issue of *Fast Company*, Cook said—

> "We change every day. We changed every day when Steve Jobs was here, and we've been changing every day since he's not been here. But the core, the values in the core, remains the same as they were in '98, as they were in '05, as they were in '10. I don't think the values should change. But everything else can change."

Southwest Airlines, an industry leader for years, has three fundamental values they use to hire, promote, and reward their employees. Those values are: A warrior's spirit, a servant's heart, and a fun-luving (their spelling) attitude.[5]

No matter how smart or technically sound you may be, if you don't possess and practice these three values, you are not likely to make it at Southwest. Or even get in the door, for that matter.

REI, the outdoor retailing co-op, made headlines one year when they decided to close on Black Friday, the day after Thanksgiving. Typically, this would be one of their strongest sales days of the year. Jerry Stritzke, REI's president and CEO at the time, explained the decision to their members in a letter:

---

5    You can find more details on each of these values at their website www.Southwest.com.

"Black Friday is the perfect time to remind ourselves of the essential truth that life is richer, more connected and complete when you choose to spend it outside. We're closing our doors, paying our employees to get out there, and inviting America to #OptOutside with us because we love great gear, but we are even more passionate about the experiences it unlocks."

REI's stores were closed on Black Friday that year. If customers went to REI's website on Black Friday to shop, they got a list of local outdoor park and trails in their area and a notice their order would not be processed until the following day. Now that's putting your money where your values are.

Tim Cook will not always be Apple's CEO. Leaders will come and go at Southwest and REI, as they do at every company. But if these companies are still around and thriving a hundred years from now, their unchanging values will be a reason.

Values are a practical tool to help navigate through difficult change.

## QUESTIONS AND TIPS FOR APPLICATION

- If you did the Two-Minute Drill as a personal exercise, summarize your results here. Based on the letter I wrote to my child, my most important values are—

---

- The Two-Minute Drill at Work: As I shared, I would not recommend doing the Two-Minute Drill in the workplace, because it is too personal. But you could try this: Instead of writing a letter to a child, have everyone imagine that they could never go to work again or ever see their colleagues again. And—after they all get done cheering!—have them write a letter describing what they would miss, and what they would want their colleagues to focus on in the future.

- Afterward, no one should be forced to share their letter or results. But for those who choose to share, it is a quick way to discover some common core values.

- My most important values at work are—

---

- Make a list of your top five core values, at work or home. Now rank them from one to five, with one being your top value. My top five values are—

  _____

  _____

  _____

  _____

- Next, do a calendar audit. Review your activities in the past few weeks. How closely do your activities align with your most important values? The activities most in line with my most important values are—

  _____

  _____

  _____

  _____

- How might you begin to integrate more activities into your routine that are consistent with your core values? The ways I will integrate my values more in my day-to-day life are—

  _____

  _____

  _____

  _____

## LATCH ON

- Values are real when you use them to make decisions.

- Values will point you in the right direction, not necessarily the easiest direction, like a compass.

- Values will alert you when you have drifted off course, like radar.

- If the values aren't right in a business deal, then the deal's not right.

PART 3

# Managing Change to Create the Life You Want

# Seven

# Imagine the Life You Want

*I FEEL LIKE A kid on the first day of school,* Brandon thought as he pulled out of the driveway. His heart was racing. *It's been a long time since I felt like this going to work. Probably almost twelve years,* he realized, *since my first day on the job at Carson-Co.*

Brandon thought about what had transpired over the last several months since he'd lost his job at Carson-Co. It hadn't been the easiest of times, but it hadn't been the worst of times either.

Getting let go had been a shock, and it took a while to adjust. But once he shifted the starting place on his Roadmap to *my new job is finding a job* and started looking forward, things had progressed fairly quickly.

Brandon had always kept up with relationships. He had regularly used his ToWho app to keep up with those who mattered most, so he had plenty of shock absorbers to help soften the blow of losing his job. Friends and family reached out to express their support, along with his former colleagues and coworkers.

In fact, it was a referral from an old boss who had left Carson-Co several years ago that led to this new opportunity. She and Brandon caught up a couple times each year. They'd get together for coffee or swap emails.

Now, even though it had been years since they had worked together directly, she was only too happy to make a connection for him. She wanted to help out Brandon because, unlike a lot of her other former colleagues, he didn't only get in touch when he needed something.

As Brandon drove, he imagined how he wanted his first day on the job to go. He had been imagining it ever since the day he had received the offer.

Brandon was a big believer in the power of using his imagination to visualize the outcomes he wanted and to make change happen for the better.

He first got the idea during a golf lesson. His golf pro had him picture a shot before he hit it. Many of the top pros practiced this technique, Brandon discovered. So he gave it a try.

To his surprise, it helped. Stepping back and imagining the path and flight of the ball worked better than just standing over the ball and taking a whack. He was still no golf pro, but his golf game had improved.

*If picturing the outcomes I want can help me in golf, maybe it can help me in other areas of my life too,* he had thought.

So Brandon began to experiment. He started imagining how he wanted to be with his wife and kids when he got home after a day searching for his new job. It was too easy to go on autopilot when he got home, to grab a beer and sit in front of the TV.

That was okay sometimes, but not always. He didn't want it to become a habit. *Family life and marriages can go stale that way,* he thought.

Brandon began imagining that he was more present with his family. During his commute home, he would think about hugging his wife and helping prepare dinner. He would anticipate shooting hoops with his daughter or helping his son with his homework.

Brandon noticed quality time with his family improved, and he became more intentional about it by using his imagination first. He used this technique as part of his job search too.

He imagined interviews before they happened. Brandon anticipated questions and imagined how he might answer them. He noticed that if he visualized himself being strong, competent, and confident ahead of time, he tended to feel and act that way in the actual interviews.

*My mind is like a computer,* he thought. *It can only do what it is programmed to do. I get to choose programs—thoughts and beliefs—that support the outcomes I want. And when I do, I am more likely to achieve them.*

If Brandon ran on autopilot, he was in danger of having his outdated programs stop him from reaching his potential. For example, getting fired had stirred up an old program or belief of his, a fear that he was not smart enough or good enough. A feeling that he should always try harder to prove himself worthy.

This particular belief acted like a computer operating system: It remained unseen, but was always running in the back of his mind. Some variation of this belief is common to many successful people.

*Who knows where that belief came from?* Brandon had wondered. *Maybe it came from comparing myself to my older brother growing up,* he thought. *Or maybe it started when Mom and Dad asked, "Why not all As?" if I came home with even one B+ on my report card.*

*He wondered if he could get the same results or even better results with a different belief.*

It did not really matter where the belief came from. It only mattered that he was aware of it now and the consequences it had in his life.

For example, trying harder to prove himself had paid off handsomely at work. Brandon often outworked his colleagues and had been rewarded with raises and promotions. That success came with a price. Often, he had little time for anything but work.

*No matter how much I did or accomplished, it never felt like enough,* he realized.

A recent comment from his wife opened his eyes. She had asked him why he was still trying to prove himself.

"You've made it. You were let go through no fault of your own, and then you worked hard until you found another job," she said. "Have you ever considered that maybe you are good enough already and don't need to prove yourself anymore?"

That was the wake-up call Brandon needed. He realized his fear of not being good enough was outdated. It was holding him back. He wondered if he could get the same results or even better results with a different belief.

He updated his computer software all the time. Wasn't it time to update his beliefs?

So Brandon created a new belief. He said to himself, "I am good enough, and I am smart enough. I don't need to prove myself to anyone anymore."

He thought about this often, especially whenever doubt crept in. It felt at forced at first, but *I am good enough* gradually became his new default operating system.

As a result, Brandon confidently walked in to his new job feeling in control of the job and, more importantly, himself.

No longer needing to prove himself allowed Brandon to take his time before acting too fast in his new role. "Listen and learn" was his mantra those first few weeks on the job. He asked questions. Lots of them.

"What is it you hope I will do coming in to this new role?" he asked.

"What is it about the culture of this place and how we do things that I need to figure out?" he asked.[6]

---

6   For more good advice on what to do coming in to a new job, check out *You're in Charge—Now What?* By Thomas J. Neff and James M. Citrin.

Through questions like these, Brandon got a clearer picture of his new colleagues' Roadmaps. Their answers helped him know where to start on his Roadmap when working with them. The weeks flew by in a blur. He was learning a lot and having fun.

*Imagining the outcomes you want is a powerful tool for making change happen.*

Late on a Friday afternoon, Brandon felt his cell phone vibrate. As he glanced down, he was startled to see the text was from *Justin*.

*Wow. I haven't heard from him in forever,* he thought.

It had been a while since Brandon had coffee with Donna.

Brandon and Donna had kept in touch some since then, but this was the first time Brandon had heard from Justin himself. He texted back, and he and Justin agreed to meet for coffee soon.

*I wonder how he's been? I wonder what he wants? I wonder why he is contacting me now?*

Brandon couldn't decide if he was more excited or scared to find out.

———

## DIG A LITTLE DEEPER:
# Imagine the Life You Want

As we saw with Brandon, imagining the outcomes you want is a powerful tool for making change happen. Imagining what you want is a kind of practice; it helps you be more prepared for new situations. [7]

### Change in Real Life: Combine Your Imagination with Passion, Patience and Persistence for Long-Term Success

When my son was six years old, he came to me and said, "Daddy, I want to play hockey."

*That's cute*, I thought. *What an imagination! Every day it's something different. He's never been on ice skates, much less played hockey. He'll forget all about it.*

But he kept asking, so I began looking for youth ice hockey programs in our city.

"Well, son," I said after a fruitless search, "I'm afraid I have some bad news for you. We live in North Carolina. Not a lot of hockey played around here."

Undaunted, standing up as tall as his four-foot-one-inch frame would allow, he looked me in the eye and declared, "Let's move to Michigan!"

I smiled. "No, we're not moving to Michigan."

His passion for hockey impressed me, so I kept looking. Eventually I told him about a youth roller hockey program I found.

---

7   For more great ideas and inspiration for tapping into the power of your imagination, check out the book *Imagine That!* by James Mapes.

"No!" he said firmly. "I want to play *ice* hockey."

Pretty impressive. This kid knew what he wanted, and he was not only passionate, he was persistent.

He came to me every few months asking, "Daddy, hockey? Daddy, hockey?"

I kept looking, but with no luck. Two years later—after a *fourth* of his life had passed—I finally saw an ad in the paper for youth ice hockey sign-ups.

"Do you still want to play?" I asked.

"Yes!" he said. So I signed him up.

The coach assured me the league was for beginners.

*They sure don't look like beginners,* I thought warily as I surveyed the locker room before his first practice.

"Hey there, son," I said to the kid getting ready next to us. "You ever play hockey before? Where you from, son?"

"Oh yes," he answered earnestly, looking up from tying his skates. "I'm from Canada!"

My kid had never been on ice skates before that moment.

*This going to be a disaster,* I thought. *He'll fall down and won't be able to get back up. All the kids will laugh. What kind of dad am I for letting him get into this predicament?*

As my son exited the locker room and waddled up to wait his turn to step onto the ice, I closed my eyes and waited for the laughter to begin. But I didn't hear anything.

I peeked. There he was, skating down the ice. I stood up.

He skated a full lap without falling down. Round and round he went. Just like all the other little kids.

*Just like he had imagined for years.*

The coach blew the whistle for drills and I cringed.

*What does my kid know about hockey drills?*

The kids got in a line; so did my son. The kid in front hit the puck and skated away, and so did my son.

I stood up taller now. The guy next to me asked, "You got a boy out there?"

"Sure do!" I said, preening now like a peacock. "Yep, my son is a hockey player."

I was full of pride (and disbelief).

"How long has he been playing hockey?" the other dad asked.

I looked at my watch. "About five minutes!"

Just like that, my son had become a hockey player.

Actually, it *wasn't* just like that. He had passionately and persistently imagined this moment for the last two years. He had been patient enough to wait for the moment to arrive.

Afterward, I gushed, "That was amazing! You looked like a hockey player out there!"

He seemed nonplussed, as if that's what he had expected.

*Because he had expected it.*

After imagining that moment scores of times over the last two years, fear never stood a chance of stopping him.

## What Are You Passionate About?

Do you have a passionate vision for your life, like my son did? Do you get up every day eager to pursue your dream? Do you have the patience and persistence to see it through, even if your initial attempts at realizing your vision turn up empty?

If not, change can be a chance to reignite your passion.

At work, it's easy to be passionate early in our careers. Everything is fresh. New. Adventurous. Things to learn. Skills to master. Mountains to climb. People to meet.

But over time, passion can fade. It's easy to fall into a pattern on your Roadmap of *"been there, done that."* Challenges become chores. Life can lose its luster at work and at home.

Imagining your future can spark new energy in your life and ignite change. How can you tap the power of your imagination to create the life you want?

## Create Your Future by Imagining It

Think about the greatest change challenge in your life right now. Maybe it's a change you want to make. Let's say your goal is to overcome a fear of public speaking. The next time you have a talk or presentation to make, you can try this beforehand.

You can try this technique while lying in bed before you go to sleep, or in the morning before you get up, or as you ride the train to work (please don't try it while you're driving!). Find a quiet place where you aren't likely to be interrupted.

Next, begin to imagine yourself giving your talk. See yourself being strong, confident, and impactful. See the audience reacting to your presence. Hear them laugh. Imagine the scene however you wish; it's your talk!

Everyone's imagination is different: When doing this exercise, you may see images like a movie, or maybe you'll just hear the words in your head, or have a feeling about giving your talk. It does not matter. Go with what works for you.

Some people may prefer to write down what they imagine. If you do, stay in the present tense. For example, you may end up writing something like this:

> *I am standing tall in front of the group. I am prepared. I have done my homework. I feel strong and confident as I scan the audience. I make eye contact as I speak. I see heads nodding in agreement to what I say. People are writing down notes. They are engaged. So am I.*

Using your imagination and mentally rehearsing before you talk may help build your confidence. The mind is a powerful computer. Why not program yours to change and create the life you want?

## QUESTIONS AND TIPS FOR APPLICATION

- Do you have a self-limiting belief from long ago that still drives your actions today? Many successful people do. What might my self-limiting belief be?

_____

_____

_____

_____

_____

- If you don't know what your self-limiting belief is, pay attention to that little voice in the back of your head. The one that says, "You should do this, and you ought to do that." Those Shoulds and Oughts may provide clues to what your program might be. My most common Shoulds and Oughts are—

_____

_____

_____

_____

_____

- Is this belief leading to some unintended consequences in your life? For example, working nonstop, having less time for family and friends, or feeling physically and emotionally run-down? If so, write down these consequences. The unintended consequences my belief is creating are—

_____

_____

_____

_____

_____

- Next, begin to imagine *intended consequences.* Start small. For example, take a moment before getting out of bed in the morning to think about how you want to be that day. See yourself thinking, feeling, and acting exactly how you want to be, whether at work or at home. Take a few moments before you leave the office to picture how you want to be when you get home. The way I want to be at work and home today is—

_____

_____

_____

_____

_____

- After you imagine your future, forget about it and go about your day. The idea is to gradually create new default programs for the computer in your mind. By periodically imagining how you want to be, gradually that belief will become your default. The new default program I will create for my life is—

_____

_____

_____

_____

- Use your imagination to prepare for specific situations. For example, if you know you have a particularly difficult conversation coming up with a colleague or coworker, take a few moments to imagine how you want the discussion to go. Visualize how you want to react before walking into the meeting. How I choose to be in this situation is—

_____

_____

_____

_____

## IMAGINE THE LIFE YOU WANT

- Imagining the life you want is the first step to achieving it.

- Your mind is like a computer and you are the programmer.

- Replace outdated programs and beliefs with new, better ones.

- Imagination, passion, patience, and persistence are your keys to long-term success.

# Eight

# Grow Where You're Planted

DONNA HAD BEEN PATIENT, but enough was enough.

*I love my husband,* she thought. *I hate to see him suffering like this. Something has to give, because I can't take it anymore. No, I won't take it anymore.*

Many months had passed since Justin had lost his job at Carson-Co. Of course it had been a big blow, and she understood that.

*It's been a big blow for all of us,* she thought. *Obviously the kids don't understand all the financial implications, but they can understand Dad hasn't been himself in a while. It's been hard on them too.*

Donna had thought long and hard about what to do. At first, she tried to be patient. She knew Justin was an emotional guy, and he was mad when he first got let go. Heck, she had been mad too. He had given Carson-Co twenty-two years of his life and had not done anything to deserve being laid off.

*But that's what happened and there is nothing we can do to change that now,* she thought. *At some point you have to move on. You have to let go. Just being mad without doing anything about it takes its toll on everyone. It's not healthy.*

After a while, she had let her anger go. But Justin was still holding on. He didn't even show signs of *wanting* to let his anger go.

*It doesn't help that he surrounds himself with others who think and act like him,* Donna realized. *If you want to move beyond something, surround yourself with those who already have.*

Donna had tried talking to him about it a couple of times. She suggested that he get out of the house more. Maybe Justin could hang around people who were more positive and moving on, like his old friend Brandon.

But Justin remained loyal to his little group of naysayers. Some of them even held on to the hope that Carson-Co would come to its senses and hire them all back. Donna thought that was delusional, but Justin said, "You never know."

Their conversations usually devolved into an argument and eventually Donna let it drop.

When things did not improve, she had begun reaching out for help. She appreciated meeting up with Brandon for coffee and advice. Just verbalizing her troubles had helped her start figuring out how to solve them. Saying things out loud seemed to crystallize her thinking. It helped issues focus.

She talked to the spouses and partners of some of the others who had been let go too and discovered that many of them were going through something similar. One of them named Juanita had shared an idea that had given Donna a new way to think about Justin's situation.

"These guys have to grow where they are planted," Juanita had said.

Donna asked, "What do you mean?"

"I get that the company treated our guys badly," Juanita answered. "That's the way it goes sometimes. Life's not always going to be fair. You have to get over it at some point and move on."

Then, Juanita showed Donna a picture.

"I look at this little plant all the time, especially when I feel sorry for myself," Juanita said. "I have a copy hanging in my kitchen."

The picture was of a young plant sprouting in concrete.

"That plant must have started out as a little seed beneath that concrete somewhere," Juanita said. "Was there any sunlight down there? No. Do you think there was much water or dirt down there? But what did that little plant do? It grew anyway! It grew where it was planted. No excuses. It found a way."

"That's a good way of looking at it," Donna said. "That's what our guys need to do now too. They need to grow where they are planted!"

Juanita said, "Now all we have to do is get them to be as smart as that plant."

The women chuckled.

"Oh, it feels good to laugh again," Donna said.

The two women realized it felt good to be around other positive people. They made arrangements to get together again soon.

As Donna walked home, she reflected on her conversation with Juanita.

*What makes us different from the plant is we* can *think. We just have to train ourselves to think in a way that gets us the outcomes that we want. This must be what Brandon has been talking about!*

He had told her a few times since their talk over coffee that imagining what you want helps you to achieve it. This idea suddenly made more sense to her. *Using your imagination is a way of thinking,* she realized.

She decided that she would use her imagination to prepare for her talks with Justin. She wanted to share the concept of "grow where you're planted" with him without it turning into another fight.

So, as she walked, Donna imagined how she might approach Justin, and how she wanted the talk to go. She pictured how he might respond, and how she could stay positive.

*I can imagine how I want our life to go, and what we're doing now isn't it. Something's got to change, and it starts with me. I'll grow where I'm planted too. I'll find a way to make it better. No excuses.*

Donna smiled at the thought.

### Change in Real Life: How to Grow Where You're Planted

When we got pregnant with our first child, my wife, Peggy, and I were thrilled.

Then, change hit like a lightning bolt out of the blue. Several months into my wife's pregnancy, the baby suddenly stopped growing. Eventually, he was born premature and with severe heart defects and several other medical problems.

Things were so dire that two days into his little life, he was nearly gone. They transferred him to a larger hospital to see what might be done. Peggy had a serious but non-life-threatening condition, and they wouldn't let her go with him. I traveled to the new hospital alone.

The attending doctor met me when I arrived and said, "Dr. Bradt, as you know, your son is very ill. He could die any minute. We don't know exactly what's wrong, but we know it has something to do with his heart. I have my best cardiologist on her way in. We'll do the best we can."

I found my way to a waiting room and sat down. My thoughts and emotions jangled together. *Why did this have to happen? It's three days before Christmas. It's not fair! What will I tell Peggy when they come to tell me that our little guy is gone?*

I was angry, scared, and alone.

Then, it hit me. The seeds of the tools I've shared in this book began to emerge out of the fog of that moment. I didn't have the language for it then, certainly; but the starting place on my Roadmap shifted to something better.

*The voice of doubt often creeps in when we face our toughest change challenges. When it does, latch on to your values, and answer it with a stronger voice.*

*What are you doing?* I thought. *Your son is down the hall fighting for his life, and you are sitting here feeling sorry for yourself? What's wrong with you?*

I had wanted to be a dad, and I was a dad, but I was failing already. Why didn't I get up and go down to where he was and be there for him? The voice of doubt had crept in, saying, "It's no use. He's going to die at any minute."

The voice of doubt often creeps in when we face our toughest change challenges. When it does, latch on to your values, and answer it with a stronger voice.

*If he might die any minute, then I better hurry up,* I thought.

I latched on to my faith, a foundation for my personal values. I prayed, *"Lord, I can't control whether my son lives or dies. That is between you and him. I will accept your will. But I promise you, for as long as you let me have him, whether it is for five minutes or five hours or five years or fifty years, I will love him with all my heart and soul, as best I can."*

With that, I let go of fear and anger and latched on to love instead. I got up and hurried down to the nurse's station. From there, I could see a crowd of doctors working over my son through a glass window. I sent him all the love my heart could muster.

By letting go of fear and latching on to love, I can't say I was happy in that moment. Far from it. But I was peaceful. I was fully present and locked in. This presence was helpful for the decision I was about to have to make.

After several hours, the doctors came out and offered me three options: We could wait and see how my son did; we could fly him to another hospital for an experimental procedure, with no guarantee it would work; or we could give him a medication that wouldn't cure anything, but might buy us some time.

"The medication option sounds good," I said. "Why don't we go with that?"

"The medication has a chance of killing him too," the doctor said. He paused, and then asked quietly, "What do you want us to do?"

The doctor waited for my answer patiently.

How do you make a decision like that? I didn't know. I'm not sure I do now. But I do know that letting go of fear and latching on to love had cleared my mind and calmed me down. I was able to stay in the moment as I considered the options.

Finally, I said, "Give him the medicine."

They did. Thankfully, miraculously, it worked. It hadn't cured anything, but it bought us some time. Eventually, my son had open-heart surgery when he was four months old. He weighed seven pounds. He survived.

Three weeks later he went into congestive heart failure, and we flew him by air ambulance back to Alabama for an emergency open-heart surgery at five months of age. He weighed six pounds. He survived.

The following months and years flew by, but change didn't slow down. He didn't eat for two years. We had to feed him through a tube in his stomach. He had cleft palate surgery, ear surgery, and hernia surgery during that time too. And a medication error during one of his hospitalizations nearly killed him.

How did Peggy and I emotionally survive during all this traumatic and continuous change? I didn't have the language for it that I have now, but we got through these hard times by putting many of the tools I've discussed in this book to use.

We changed our Roadmaps to focus on what we could control, instead of what we could not. We let go of fear and latched on to love, and we latched on to values born of our faith. We were fortunate to have relationships to act as shock absorbers. We were surrounded with love and support from friends, family, and even strangers along the way.

And we latched on to our sense of humor whenever we could. Humor is a wonderful tool to break the tension of change, as we will explore more in the Afterword.

At one point during all this, my wife quipped, "If this kid survives, he's either going to grow up to be a doctor or a serial nurse killer!"

We were incredibly fortunate. Our son survived all that and grew up to become that little hockey player I told you about in chapter seven.

Today, my son is a young man that I love with all my heart and soul, just as I had promised during my prayer. As I write this, he is about to get married. And he is one of the best teachers I have ever had.

My son did not choose the circumstances of his birth. He was born with the odds stacked against him. But fortunately, he was too young to think *woe is me* or to indulge in self-pity. Instead, he put every ounce of energy he had into surviving and taking his next breath.

Like that little plant, he grew where he was planted. He found a way, no excuses. And by watching him, I learned I could choose to do the same, whenever change hits and affects my life.

And so can you. I hope his story inspires you to grow where you're planted whenever change turns your life upside down, too.

## QUESTIONS AND TIPS FOR APPLICATION

Think about the toughest change challenge you face right now:

- See if you can find someone to talk to, like Donna did. Sometimes verbalizing your thoughts and feelings helps clarify them and gives you an idea of what to do next. The people I will talk to about this change are—

_____

_____

_____

_____

- Do you surround yourself with positive people who encourage you to move forward? Do you find yourself more encouraged or discouraged after spending time with them? Try minimizing the time you spend around negative people or folks who bring you down. Sometimes moving on means leaving behind those who prefer to stay stuck or blame others for their plight.

- The people I will choose to spend time with going forward are—

_____

_____

_____

_____

- Sometimes opportunity is right in front of us but we miss it. As you think about your current situation, where might the opportunity lie? Is there an opportunity to learn? To inspire others? To offer love and support to someone else? To accept love and support from others? To take your life or career in a new direction? To learn a new skill? Or something else perhaps? Try not to let the pain or difficulties of your situation blind you to the opportunity that may be staring you in the face. The opportunities this change has created for me are—

_____

_____

_____

_____

- Sometimes opportunity becomes clear only in retrospect. For example, if you had told me during the lowest point of my son's ordeal that, long term, this experience would launch me on a new career as a speaker and a writer and his story would help a lot of people, well, I might have punched you! But long term, that's exactly what happened. If I let myself dream, the potential long-term opportunities from this change might be—

_____

_____

_____

_____

## GROW WHERE YOU'RE PLANTED

- Sometimes change, and life, are not fair.

- Grow where you're planted. Find a way. No excuses.

- Surround yourself with positive people.

- Finding opportunity may begin with believing it is there.

*Nine*

# Write Your Story

"I PROPOSE A TOAST!" Kimberly exclaimed, raising her glass of champagne high in the air. "To the new Carson-Co!"

"To the new Carson-Co!" her team cried out in unison. Kimberly scanned the large crowd of faces smiling back at her. Some faces were familiar and many were new.

It had been a year since the deal had gone through and the two former competitors had gone to market together. Kimberly had gathered her team tonight to celebrate their accomplishments.

"We have come a long way on our journey, and we still have a long way to go," Kimberly said, "but if we keep working together, with our common vision and common values bonding us together, nothing can stop us!"

"Hear, hear!" someone shouted.

"Winston Churchill once said, 'History will be kind to me, because I intend to write it,'" Kimberly said. "Well, since we have come together, we have begun to write our own history. I like the story so far. How about you?"

More cheers rang out.

"And"—her voice built to a crescendo now—"I can't wait to see how the story ends! And we get to write it!"

More cheers all around.

"Hear, hear!"

Ken stood in the back of the room, smiling as he took it all in.

*She has come a long way in the past year,* he thought. *She's grown from being an individual contributor to leading a team of contributors.*

Ken knew that wasn't always an easy transition for a leader to make. *I've known many who have stayed comfortable by doing what they've always done. She took a chance and changed. It paid off.*

Kimberly's work on the Culture Transition Team had impressed the new owners. They noticed her collaborative approach to leadership. And they liked her team's recommendations for creating a new company culture, instead of trying to preserve sacred cows from their past.

The owners offered Kimberly a role in the new organization, and she had attacked it with her usual zeal. Ken was particularly impressed with how she had staffed it.

*She looked for the best talent she could find,* he thought. *That's why she's here celebrating tonight. She didn't surround herself with only her buddies, or the people she liked, or the folks who made her feel comfortable.*

"We need to challenge and learn from one another," Kimberly had said when selecting her team. "We need to make each other uncomfortable a bit. That's how we are going to continue to innovate, grow, and change as an organization."

It was through the Culture Transition Team that the new owners became aware of Cheryl, too. Her leadership skills impressed them, and they asked her if she had ever worked in human resources before.

"No," she said, "I've dabbled in finance, but I have been in operations most of my career."

"That's perfect," they responded. "We need people in HR who understand the business and act as partners with the business leaders, instead of just serving as the policy police. We need to embed a culture of 'One Carson-Co' across the new company."

They told her that they were bringing in a new executive vice president of HR.

*Their biggest risk was doing nothing.*

"We'd like you to talk with her about becoming our new chief leadership and culture officer," they said.

Cheryl was shocked, "I am honored, but I am not sure what a chief leadership and culture officer does."

"Neither do we!" they had responded. "We've never had one before, but we it's apparent we need one now, and you are just the person for the job."

Cheryl quickly learned that this was the way the new owners thought and operated. The starting place on their Roadmap was always "adapt first and fast." They believed they could always backtrack or pivot to something better if needed. The one thing they couldn't afford to do was stand still.

When they decided to move on something, they didn't waste a lot of time doing exhaustive studies to cover their backsides in case it didn't pan out. They weren't reckless about it, but they allowed common sense to take precedence over caution when warranted.

They viewed their biggest risk as doing nothing at all. They understood the world around them was changing too fast for that.

*No wonder they were always ahead of the market,* Cheryl thought. *They aren't afraid to experiment and take chances. If something doesn't work, they simply learn from the experience and quickly move on.*

*You can't make a change if you don't take a chance.*

Cheryl was inspired by their approach. She took the interview and got the job. It was not a role she had envisioned, but it reinforced something she had learned early in her career: You can't make a change if you don't take a chance.

Cheryl and Edward applied this principle to their family life too. They went away for a long weekend without the kids to think about how they would manage the demands her new role would make on their family.

Now that her parents lived closer by, it was easier for Cheryl and Edward to get out more. Her parents were happy to babysit occasionally and see their grandkids more often. Cheryl could assist her parents more easily now, too, when they needed it. It was a win-win all the way around. The move to a senior living facility could wait.

During their weekend away, Cheryl and Edward decided that he would ask for a role at work that would allow him to travel less. The only position available was a part-time role, but he took it.

They calculated that Cheryl's new salary would help with the difference in income. It was close enough anyway. If they needed to crimp here or there, so be it.

They had decided it was better to have a little less and enjoy the life they had than to have more money and be too busy to enjoy it anyhow.

For now, this decision gave Edward more time at home and provided more stability for the family.

Like any new change, it felt uncomfortable at first. There was a period of adjustment for everyone. But soon, Edward being home more and assuming more household duties was normal. Before long, everyone had settled into the new routine.

Across town, Brandon was happily doing the same.

He was enjoying his new job like never before. Being freed from the pressure to prove himself had made him more effective. He explained his new approach to a friend one night over dinner.

"I used to think I always had to outwork everyone else to prove my worth," he said. "It worked to a degree, but at a price. Some of my colleagues thought I was overly aggressive, and my family hardly saw me at all. Any satisfaction I felt from getting promoted faded fast, because I immediately began fighting for the next one. And no matter what I did, it never felt like enough. It was exhausting."

So this time, Brandon decided he was going to let go of worrying about getting promoted and stop comparing himself to everyone else. Instead, he wanted to enjoy the role he had, work hard, do the best he could, then go home and enjoy his family.

"How's it working out?" his friend asked.

Brandon laughed. "Ever since I decided that, I've been getting promoted like crazy!"

Shortly after that dinner, Brandon had caught up with Justin over coffee too. As was his style, Justin had gotten right to the point.

Justin told Brandon that his talk with Donna was a real wake-up call.

"She didn't pull any punches. She let me know how hard this has been on her and the kids too," Justin said. "She made me realize I got so wrapped up in my problems I had ignored theirs."

Donna had also told Justin she was no longer willing to put her life on hold waiting for him to get over his job loss. She was going to see a family counselor to help her and the kids move on emotionally, and if he wanted to join her, great. But she was going to go for help regardless.

"Wow, good for her," Brandon responded. "Strong message. How did you take it?"

"Well, not so good at first," Justin admitted. "I can be pretty hardheaded, you know."

"Tell me about it," Brandon said with a warm grin. Justin gave a quick nod in agreement.

"But after taking some time to think it through, I realized she was right. I was stuck and going nowhere," Justin admitted. "I finally understood it was time to move on."

Justin paused and grabbed for his coffee. It was hard him to feel vulnerable.

"That's why I reached out to you, Brandon. I'm not here to ask for a job or favors or anything. Donna suggested I start hanging out with different people, more positive people, and I think she is right."

Justin had realized that hanging around negative people only brought him down.

"I used to enjoy hanging out with you some, so anyhow, I'm hoping we can start spending more time together again, I guess is what I'm trying to say."

Brandon was touched. "I appreciate that, Justin. I would enjoy that too. Maybe we can coach together again? Soccer season is just around the corner, you know."

"That would be great," Justin said as he took a sip of his coffee. He paused as if to take it all in.

"Yeah, that would be great."

Then he added: "Well, wait a minute. I guess there is one favor I wanted to ask of you after all."

Brandon's ears perked up, "What's that?"

Justin leaned forward.

"I just remembered something Donna told me to ask you about. Some sort of new age BS idea around imagining the life you want or something like that," he said with a smile.

"Do you really want to know, or are you just messing around?" Brandon asked. With Justin it was sometimes hard to tell.

"Yeah, I want to know," Justin said. "I told you I'm ready to change. Whatchya got?"

*I guess when the mind is ready a teacher will appear,* Brandon thought.

"Happy to oblige, Justin. I discovered this idea when I took some golf lessons, believe it or not . . ."

The reunited friends ended up talking deep into the night.

## DIG A LITTLE DEEPER:
## The Five Choices of Change

We don't always get to choose change, but we always get to choose our response to it. There are five basic choices we can make in response to change.

## THE FIVE CHOICES OF CHANGE

1. Hold On or Let Go

2. Forgive or Find Blame

3. Run Toward or Away

4. Believe in Opportunity or Believe in Bad Luck

5. Risk Moving On or Risk Staying Put

I hope that as we have watched Cheryl and all the others we met learn how to adapt to and advance through change in their lives with their choices, that you have too.

## QUESTIONS AND TIPS FOR APPLICATION

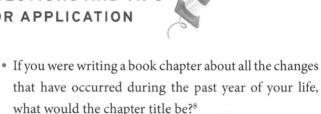

- If you were writing a book chapter about all the changes that have occurred during the past year of your life, what would the chapter title be?[8]

_____

_____

_____

_____

- Is this story turning out as you had hoped? If so, how?

_____

_____

_____

---

8    A great idea I got from the Learning and Development folks at PwC, PriceWaterhouseCoopers.

- If the story is turning out as you wish, great. Continue having fun writing the story. If not, following are some ideas to help you change by writing a new story.

## WRITING YOUR NEW STORY

- Choose a chapter title for the next six months of your life. Choose a title that inspires you: a forward-looking, optimistic title. The title I choose for the next six months of my life is—

_____

_____

_____

- Think about that title and imagine thinking, feeling, acting, and getting the results the title implies. To create my life over the next six months, I will—

_____

_____

_____

_____

- Imagining the life you want is the first step to creating it. Begin living the story every day. The one thing I will do today to advance my story is—

_____

_____

_____

_____

## WRITE YOUR STORY

- You are the author of your life story.

- You don't always get to choose how your change story begins, but you always get to choose how it ends.

- What will the next chapter of your change story be?

# Afterword

## It's All Bubblicious

I had a client who was scared to death she would make a mistake. Her job was not one with life or death consequences, but it felt like that to her.

I asked her to think about her fear and how she could get over it. I loved what she came back with.

She replied, "I decided it's like this: If I ran a convenience store and made a mistake, say I did not order enough Bubblicious one month, I'd just order more Bubblicious the next month. I wouldn't get all worked up over it."

I exclaimed, "You got it. It's *all* Bubblicious. Life is serious enough without us piling on and making it worse!"

Change can be hard. Sometimes, like with my son, change does have life-or-death consequences. But as we saw, even then there is room for humor. In fact, humor is a practical tool many smart and effective leaders employ to lessen the tension around change.

They realize humor goes beyond just keeping things in perspective. It also opens the mind, relaxes the body, and implies to followers, "*We got this.*"

Let's consider Abraham Lincoln. Perhaps no one has ever had a tougher job or had to deal with more dramatic, high-stakes change then he did when the Civil War began shortly after he took office. The future of the country Lincoln was elected to lead hung in the balance.

The war went poorly for Lincoln at first because his generals were hesitant to fight. Finally, General Ulysses S. Grant stepped to the fore and fought well. Grant quickly got on Lincoln's radar.

Just as quickly, the rumor mill began, as it does today when people think that someone has begun to surpass their peers.

*You didn't hear it from me, but Grant has a drinking problem. Does the president know that Grant has a drinking problem? You might want to pass that on.*

Indeed, history is ambiguous. Grant may or may not have had an actual drinking problem.

Regardless, Lincoln's purported response to the rumors went something like this:

> "My gosh, the only general I have who will fight and win battles has a drinking problem? What are we to do? I'll tell you what. Find out what he drinks. Send a barrel of it to all my other generals. I need this man. At least he will fight!"

By all accounts, Lincoln suffered greatly from depression and melancholy over the course of his life, especially during the last few tortuous years of the war, but he never lost his sense of humor. He often responded to his colleagues' queries with a humorous story or anecdote to make a point and to help break the tension.

*It's how we choose to adapt to change that makes all the difference.*

Lincoln's example reminds us that change leaders take their jobs seriously. They take the needs of others seriously. But they rarely, if ever, take themselves too seriously.

## Adapt and Advance

As we have seen throughout this book, unpredictable change really is predictable. We don't always know when change will happen or how, but we know it will.

Therefore, going through change does not make us, or the organizations we work for, unique. Rather, it's how we choose to adapt to change that makes all the difference.

I hope this book helps you adapt and advance whenever change unexpectedly affects your life. And I hope you will share what you have learned with those you live with and work with. We are all on this change journey together, and in the end, that's what makes it all worthwhile.

# About the Author

WHEN GARY BRADT'S FIRST child was born with a life-threatening heart condition, it forced him to learn to adapt to difficult and unwanted change. He has since gone on to dedicate his career to helping others adapt to change in their lives too, both at work and at home.

A clinical psychologist and executive coach, Gary got his start as a speaker on change when Dr. Spencer Johnson chose him to be the leading speaker worldwide for Johnson's phenomenal best seller *Who Moved My Cheese*? Gary has since shared his message on change for organizations like IBM, JP Morgan Chase, eBay, and scores of others.

Through his work as a speaker, writer, and coach, Gary hopes that others will come to discover as he has: It is not the change in our lives, but how we choose to adapt to it, that makes all the difference.

You can follow him on LinkedIn and on Twitter @GaryBradt. More information on his speaking is available at www.garybradt.com.